THE HISTORY OF CATHOLIC CHURCH MUSIC

KARL GUSTAV FELLERER

The History of
Catholic Church Music

Translated by
FRANCIS A. BRUNNER, C.Ss.R.

GREENWOOD PRESS, PUBLISHERS
WESTPORT, CONNECTICUT

Library of Congress Cataloging in Publication Data

Fellerer, Karl Gustav, 1902-
  The history of Catholic Church music.

  Translation of Geschichte der katholischen Kirchen-
musik.
  Reprint of the ed. published by Helicon Press,
Baltimore.
  Bibliography: p.
  Includes index.
  1. Church music--Catholic Church--History and
criticism. I. Title.
[ML3002.F32 1979]   783'.026'209   78-21637
ISBN 0-313-21147-7

Nihil Obstat: EDWARD A. CERNY, S.S., S.T.D.
             Censor Librorum
Imprimatur: ✠ FRANCIS P. KEOUGH, D.D.
             Archbishop of Baltimore
             September 26, 1961

The *Nihil Obstat* and *Imprimatur* are official declarations that a book or pamphlet is free of doctrinal or moral error. No implication is contained therein that those who have granted the *Nihil Obstat* and *Imprimatur* agree with the opinions expressed.

This is an authorized translation of the second edition of *Geschichte der katholischen Kirchenmusik*, published in Düsseldorf Musikverlag Schwann in 1949.

Reprinted with the permission of Helicon Press, Inc.

Reprinted in 1979 by Greenwood Press
A division of Congressional Information Service, Inc.
88 Post Road West, Westport, Connecticut 06881

Library of Congress Catalog Card Number 78-21637

ISBN 0-8371-21147-7

Printed in the United States of America

10 9 8 7 6 5 4 3 2

Translator's Preface

Music is far more important in divine service than many seem to think. It is not just a fine but unnecessary ornament of the liturgy; it is, in the words of Pope St. Pius X, a functional part — *parte integrante* — of divine worship, serving both the glory of God and the edification of the faithful. Ideally, sacred music is the handmaiden of the liturgy, wholly absorbed in the service of the altar. But in fact it is sometimes divorced from such service and apparently made an end in itself. Principles governing its adaptation to the liturgy are at times forgotten or neglected, and music is allowed to go its own way, disregarding ritual law or even ritual propriety. Through the years, then, music has played a fluctuating role. To trace the varied and various relationships of music to the liturgy in the twenty centuries of Catholic Church history is the task Professor Fellerer sets for himself.

It is a formidable task, and only a man of Fellerer's special competence could hope to sketch a work that would be complete without being exhaustive. Years of lecturing at the University of Fribourg (Switzerland) and in Cologne have served as a background for the present volume.

Fellerer is keenly aware that it is not enough to outline the progress of the musical arts; they must also be placed in their proper perspective, must be seen in their relationship to the function they are supposed to perform, must be judged according to the fulfillment of their assigned roles. This book is not concerned so much with individual composers and their personal artistic development as with their contribution to the musical currents and their links with the milieu in which they worked. The book endeavors to follow the movements characteristic of each epoch, along with the continued fortunes of traditional forms. In church music the old and the new are found side by side.

Of course a volume like this serves only as a survey, but it is far from superficial. Professor Fellerer manages to incorporate the major findings of scholarly research without burdening the reader with the trappings of the scholar's apparatus. This is no mean achievement, and it is left to the reader to judge for himself how successfully the task has been accomplished.

This translation was made from the second (revised) edition of 1949, but the translator has had the benefit of additional notes and corrections supplied by Dr. Fellerer. The paragraphs dealing with church music on the American scene have been augmented by Miss Joan Boucher, to whom the translator is indebted also for a careful reading and correction of the whole typescript.

The translator owes a great debt of gratitude to Rev. Richard Schuler for his painstaking revision of the entire typescript; if this translation has any merit, it is due in large measure to his helpful and valuable suggestions.

FRANCIS A. BRUNNER, C.SS.R.

discusses

Contents

THE HISTORY OF CATHOLIC CHURCH MUSIC

Introduction

LITURGICAL PURPOSE OF CATHOLIC CHURCH MUSIC

Catholic church music is circumscribed by its place in the divine service; the limits of its expression and its forms are clearly set by the shape of the liturgy. By this extramusical limitation it is distinguished, as practical art, from sacred music that is solely a free expression of religious feeling. This liturgical purpose also gives it its particular denominational character. In the Protestant service, church music adopted certain forms that made it fundamentally Protestant. In the Catholic service, church music is not merely an ornament, but a basic part of the liturgy. Changes in our way of thinking through the centuries have often made this relationship of music to the forms of divine service appear indistinct, but its purpose has always been definitely outlined. As a result there has at times been a cleavage or a tension between the aim of Catholic church music and its evaluation and production by men whose roots are deep in their own age and their own land. Wherever art has a well-defined purpose, this tension between the aim and the actualization of this aim is much to the fore, and it restricts and conditions the distinct development of that art.

CHURCH MUSIC AND ART

A second basic purpose of Catholic church music is to be found in its distinctive artistic character. Music is an expression of artistic feelings.

1

The multiplicity of its forms of expression can be traced to different national and racial origins and to a variety of human experiences. In every type of music the cultural background as well as the century have left their influences on the forms employed. Church music is inherently restricted by its practical purpose of being composed for a service. But there have been periods in its history when that purpose was overshadowed by the musical art itself, which was given free rein, and the restrictions imposed upon it by the liturgy were forgotten. Any consideration of the historical evolution of Catholic church music must distinguish the music of worship from religious music in general and take into account the changes in artistic expression, as well as the changes in liturgical conception and attitude that occurred through the centuries.

PRACTICAL CHURCH MUSIC

The peculiar character of practical church music presupposes a variety of problems which differ according to circumstances. Cathedral choirs or choirs in large monastic establishments have different resources than the choir in a simple country parish. A historical description of church music as a utilitarian art demands that practical conditions be considered, for these will often yield a picture that differs widely from that of the art as a whole. Practical considerations, with the demands that arise from time and place, determine the development of church music to a great degree. Where conditions are poor and where a purely musical bent of minds is lacking, these practical considerations are felt even more strongly. This is demonstrated by the varying attitudes toward Gregorian chant. Liturgy and music are opposite poles between which the changes in church music through the centuries take place, depending on whether the emphasis falls on one or on the other.

THE LITURGICAL FUNCTION IN HISTORY

The relation of music to its liturgical function is the central question in the development of church music in all periods of its history. Questions of musical evolution as well as historical tradition are both subordinated to it. The meaning of the liturgy is established by ecclesiastical authority, but its interpretation and its understanding are determined by men whose roots are deep in time and place and popular background; interpretation and understanding are therefore subject to change. Thus church music in various countries and at various times has differed in its media and its attitude toward the liturgical action.

When the liturgy was being formed in the first Christian centuries there was no difficulty or disagreement, because the musical expression grew with, and out of, the liturgical form. As liturgical song, church music was the music of the liturgy in the fullest meaning of that phrase. It was the music *of* worship. It was not until church music became an independent art and went its own way in the effort to enhance the inner liturgical expression with artistic means that any problem arose regarding the place of music in worship; for church music must determine both its relationship to religious content and to liturgy as well as its relationship to musical development in general. Church music became music *for* worship. The development of free melodic forms and polyphony, which took a secular direction as well as an ecclesiastical one, produced an artistic development within the divine service. In the stylistic compromise of Palestrina, music achieved both its highest ecclesiastical and its highest artistic shape in the divine service. The cultural development outside the Church since the Renaissance and Humanism, and the assumption of leadership by secular music, were the chief reasons for an encroachment upon church music by a subjective art of expression and an emotional creativity. The result was music *at* worship based on extraecclesiastical artistic principles. The independence of church music in the divine service during the second period of development, when the break in unity between liturgy and ecclesiastical song began, led during the third period to an almost total separation of church music from its liturgical foundation. But reforms in church music, and new conceptions in ecclesiastical and artistic spheres during the nineteenth century, brought music and liturgy together in a new inner relationship that became the basis for the present state of church music.

VARIOUS PHASES IN CHURCH MUSIC

Thus in the historical course of church music four large periods of development are marked off. But the phases in these manifold currents and countercurrents shift from one center to another in time and place and often opposite movements are found side by side, complicated further by the continuing force of traditions and by ecclesiastical and artistic discussion. Differences in intellectual conditions in various localities in the broad Christian world produce differences in artistic expression. The variety of racial backgrounds in many cultural areas not only produces a different musical language from period to period, but also a different attitude toward worship, liturgy, and church music. The readiness in various cultural areas to adopt and adapt borrowed or acquired forms gives rise, even within a temporary stylistic development, to knotty questions concerning the general intellectual and artistic attitudes of peoples and races. On this basis Gregorian chant, although an obligatory part of church-music culture in every period and in every locality, has had as many adaptations as the vernacular hymn when transplanted by colonists and missionaries. This exchange of characteristically national forms of artistic expression is found in all periods.

CHURCH MUSIC AND GENERAL MUSICAL DEVELOPMENT

In every century church music has been an essential part of musical life. Fluctuations have existed in every age in the relationship between church music and secular music, and it is impossible to reduce the matter to a simple formula such as: in the Middle Ages church music was on the giving end; in modern times, on the receiving end. Religious music has always had its influence on religious experience, while church music has always had a purpose and task that links it on the one hand with liturgy, and on the other with people. A church music estranged from the people conforms as little to the genuine idea of church music as one that is purely externalized and estranged from liturgy. The presentation and evaluation of church music is therefore determined not only from the standpoint of artistic development but also from the position it occupies in relation to its ecclesiastical purpose and its reception by the people. Hence any historical consideration of church music must have a perspective different from that requisite for a consideration of phenomena purely musical and secular.

TRADITIONAL FORMS IN CHURCH MUSIC

There is still another point in which the history of church music differs from the history of independent musical forms. Many of the liturgical types developed in the course of history still survive, whereas most secular musical forms developed contemporaneously are no longer a part of musical life. But this tradition conceals certain dangers for any historical consideration: for a present-day evaluation is far too easily injected into the consideration of the past and thus the meaning of the historical reality is clouded. A true historical method must represent and evaluate ancient art in the spirit of its own age; its present-day value is a question that belongs to another sphere. Church-music life in every era was characterized by the cultivation both of new music and the old historical forms. Therefore the attitude of past generations towards the historical forms of Gregorian chant and classic polyphony is of real value for study and is as important as understanding their position regarding musical development in general. Likewise, because it is the handmaid of the liturgy and a practical art, church music has had its own conditions for development, as well as its own history of progress.

CHURCH AND MUSIC

The Church has always regarded music as an integral part of worship and so has always given it close attention. In the Old and New Testaments, as well as in the writings of the fathers, questions of church music were discussed. Popes Celestine (423–432), Leo (444–461), Gelasius I (492–496), and Hormisdas (514–523) were deeply interested in promoting church music. Gregory I (590–604) ordered the training of singers for church, as well as the arrangement of the chants, which were declared obligatory by Pope Leo III (847–855). The councils of Laodicea (343–381), Venice (465), Toledo (589), Mainz (813), Aachen (816), Rome (835) and others enacted prescriptions concerning church music that were re-enacted and expanded by other councils in the centuries that followed. The Rule of St. Chrodegang, the *Instituta Patrum* (10th c.), as well as other medieval writings, complete the exposition of the Church's position regarding church music.

When new problems arose with the introduction of polyphony, Pope John XXII, in his constitution *Docta Ss. Patrum* (1324), took cognizance of them by means of official ordinances. Pope Marcellus II (1555), as well as the Council of Trent (1546–1563), distinguished between church music and profane compositions. Numerous provincial synods followed this pattern. Popes Urban VIII (1623–1644), Alexander VII (1655–1667), Innocent XI (1676–1689), and Innocent XII (1691–1700) issued orders in view of the new musical development. The *Caeremoniale episcoporum* (1600), like the medieval *Ordines*, summarized the tasks of church music. In his encyclical *Annus qui* (1749), Pope Benedict XIV (1740–1758) issued new regulations in view of contemporary musical ideas.

The ecclesiastical reform of the nineteenth century occasioned many discussions regarding church music, for the most part about the Gregorian chant. In the brief, *Multum ad movendos animos* (1870), Pope Pius IX confirmed the establishment of the Caecilian Society as chief agent of the reform movement, especially in German-speaking countries.

But it was in the present century that the movement for reform bore its best fruit. In the motu proprio, *Inter pastoralis officii* (1903), Pope St. Pius X created a comprehensive summary of existing church-music legislation whose prescriptions were reaffirmed by the *Codex juris canonici* (1917). In the apostolic constitution, *Divini cultus sanctitatem* (1928), Pope Pius XI renewed the basic ideas of the motu proprio. Pope Pius XII, in his encyclical, *Mediator Dei* (1947), gave music its rightful place in the liturgy and in his encyclical, *Musicae sacrae disciplina* (1955), he emphasized the cultural task of religious music and the importance of the contemporary church-music composer. Musical training in the seminary and the work of musical research were both given special attention. Finally, on September 3, 1958, the Sacred Congregation of Rites issued a series of directives regulating sacred music, especially in relation to popular participation in the liturgy.

I Music of Worship

CHAPTER 1

The Development of
Liturgical Chant

BEGINNINGS AND FIRST PHASE OF CHRISTIAN CHURCH MUSIC

The history of Catholic church music begins with the early development and spread of Christianity. The natural expression of prayer in song, using an appropriate musical form, was already present in the time of Christ. Holy Writ recounts that at the Last Supper the Hallel (Pss. 113–118 and Pss. 134–136) was sung, and the Acts of the Apostles hint at the festive character of early Christian worship. Appropriate songs were taken into the Christian service, and as Christianity spread, the liturgical forms adopted local melodic peculiarities. Those who preached Christianity brought with them their songs, but the new communities of Christians praised the Lord in their own fashion. Thus arose the different chants and liturgies of the various churches, Syrian, Greek-Alexandrian, Byzantine, East and West Syrian, Coptic, Abyssinian, Armenian and Roman. The development of the rites and chants of these different liturgies led to further evolution in their liturgical chants in the course of the centuries. Thus the Byzantine liturgy took on both Greek and Slavic forms under Cyril (✠869) and Methodius (✠885), as it spread into new areas. Each area of liturgical development produced distinctive melodic settings, so that just as the rites themselves show differences traceable to their places of origin, so also the music manifested local differences of form.

9

Byzantine Hymn (Mon. Mus. Byz. Transcr. Vol. I, S. 96)

'Α - φθό - ρου τό - κου Μα - ρί - ας ὑπ - άρ - χων

μάρ - τυς κα - τα - γώ - γι - ον ἀ - λήκτως πέ - λων

ἐν φω - τὶ ἀ - ύ - λω - τε καὶ ἡ - μῖν

εὐ - με - - νί ζου Τρι - ά - δα ἅ - κτι - στον.

Syrian melodies influenced the Byzantine chant which in turn greatly influenced the whole of the Mediterranean basin. The spread of Byzantine Christianity brought its songs to the most distant places. The Oxyrhynchos hymn is an early example of Byzantine church music found in Egypt.

Tune of an Armenian Church hymn

Hor - hurt me - z iev es - kan - cie - li _____ vor

hai - sm a - vur haid - ne - tzav ho - virkn

ier - ken en_____ t hrësh-da_____gs dan

a _____ ve _____ dis ash - ha_____r - hi

Oxyrhynchos Fragment, 3rd century

... υ - τα - νη - ω　　σι γά　τω μηδ' ἄ - στρα φα - έ - σφο-

ρα λει-πέσθων ... πο - τα - μῶν　ῥο - θί - ων　πᾶ - σαι　ὑμ - νούν-

των δ'ἡ - μῶν πα - τέ - ρα　χ'υί - ὸν　χ' ἅ - γι - ον　πνεῦ - μα

πᾶ - σαι δυ - νά - μεις έ - πι - φω - νούν - των ἀ - μὴν　　ἀ - μὴν

κρά - τος　αἰ - νος . . .　　　δω - τῆ-

ρι μό - νῳ πάν - των ἀγα - θῶν ἀ - μὴν　ἀ - μὴν.

The widespread diffusion of the Byzantine tradition in the Mediterranean area could not but have an influence on Latin church music.

THE ROMAN ECCLESIASTICAL CHANTS

The variety of forms in the rites and chants of the Eastern Church stands in marked contrast to the unified evolution of the forms of worship and singing of the Church in the West. The central position held by Rome was bound to impress that church's own type of music on the whole area. Activity in church music reached a high point in Rome in the sixth century. Various influences from the East by way of Alexandria and Greece combined with the local musical culture to produce a body of liturgical chants used in Rome before the reforms of St. Gregory the Great. In view of the strong tradition regarding the revisions undertaken by this reform pope, it is impossible not to speak of a "Gregorian chant"; but what precise form of extant chant *is* the product of this reform? The surviving so-called Old Roman chant may not really be a remnant of pre-Gregorian chant but rather the form revamped by Gregory or even later, at the end of the seventh century. On the other hand, what we call the traditional Gregorian chant — the form that is reconstructed in the Vatican editions — may actually represent not the Gregorian reform but a radical revision undertaken later, during the pontificates of Martin (649–655) and especially Vitalian (657–672), or even the development necessitated by the transfer to Frankish territories. All this remains a moot problem. At any rate it is the latter form that occupied the forefront in the development of the music of the Western church. Thus not only the liturgical forms but the various musical traditions of the many lands where Christianity made contact were absorbed and lost, except for a few fragmentary remnants.

The condition of music in Italy complicated this adjustment, because its origins lay in a variety of places and social strata. It was partly oriental, but there was also a component of the general Mediterranean culture; it was partly Italian, but it was also adapted to the rationalism of an overrefined Greek culture. Christianity first took root among the lower classes. These people established the basic forms of liturgical music and made possible the adoption of a store of melodies derived from the Orient and from the common Mediterranean culture. These melodies were in use in many congregations. They were the expression of the new Christian attitude of prayer, which was carefully protected from the danger of secularization through pagan music.

THE EXPRESSION OF CULT

As a result of the Edict of Milan (313) granting toleration to the Church, religious ritual expanded. General Christian beliefs, as well as a spiritualized conception of music, became known to wider circles. This religious attitude had the strength to clear away the remnants of ancient pagan musical life. The Church adopted what was good, revised it, and gave it new spiritual meaning. Thus the way was gradually prepared for a new religious foundation for musical life. Primitive Italian Christianity had the task of preserving both the purity of the doctrines of faith, and the musical expression of that faith; in other words, it was faced with the problem of adopting only that portion of the existing musical practice that could serve as an expression of an inviolable faith, and of rejecting the rest. The "worship in spirit" (Jn. 4:23), with its implied rejection of a purely esthetic enjoyment of music, was the basis for the general repudiation of instrumental music, customary in pagan worship. Although certain forms of instrumental playing and women's singing were permitted by some, most held that only "singing in the heart" is prayer, as the Apostle Paul (Eph. 5:19; Col. 3:16) avers. Worship, and with it the music of worship, is a spiritual activity; it is cult and not art. The thought of merely singing "at" worship was alien to early Christian thinking. Music either must participate in worship or it has no part. Hence the systematic opposition to pagan sacrificial music, so clearly emphasized by Clement of Alexandria, Tertullian, Arnobius and others, was based firmly on this new spiritual attitude of Christianity.

The basis of Christian ecclesiastical music was its vocal character. It was the prayer of the community sung by the people. Because of the emphasis on the "spiritual community" in the worship of the first two centuries, men and women joined in the singing. But the spiritual relaxation that followed the outward expansion of Christianity presented serious difficulties for maintaining a unified cult. Thus the singing of women fell into disrepute, especially after the heretics exercised such an attraction by using women's choirs for the performance of hymns. St. Ambrose approved of women's singing, particularly in psalmsinging, where "tender maidens can let their tuneful voices rise without damage to their womanly modesty, and virgins and widows without danger to morality." In the fourth century, by such writings as the *Didascalia*, and the works of St. Isidore of Pelusium, and others, the restriction on women's singing was linked chiefly with the danger of heresy and immorality. The Council of Auxerre (578) gave the prohibition of women's singing general force. As a result, both the unity of the congregation at worship and community singing were destroyed. By ordaining boy choristers to the order of lector, the singing was now generally given to clerics, thus giving a special position to church singers.

CHRISTIAN AND ANCIENT PAGAN MUSICAL VIEWS

The liberation of Christianity in the fourth century created two problems that at first appeared contradictory: the one was the internal consolidation of the Church's musical life, with its growing exclusion of secular (pagan) music; the other was the necessary adjustment to the intellectual forces of ancient music and the task of injecting them with a Christian spirit.

A clarification was made necessary by the situation in which the Church found itself as a result of its new position as the state religion under Constantine the Great (324–337). The inner spiritual preparation for the faith or its outward expression was no longer as general among Christians as in the days of the catacombs; the danger of falling back into heathen ways of thinking was much stronger among the masses who began to stream into the Church than it had been in primitive Christianity with its profound spirituality. Even then there had been difficulty in trying to inject a Christian spirit into existing customs and musical practices, as the exhortations of the apostles and fathers show. Therefore this endless stream, coming into the Church without the difficult inner and outer probation that the Christians of the catacombs had undergone, had to be accustomed all the more carefully to Christian ways of thinking by the removal of all heathen practices they had grown fond of. For this reason instrumental music and women's singing, as well as melodies current in pagan use, had to be withheld from divine service.

Although Christian musical endeavor shut itself off from the ancient art of its time, since this was a danger for the newly established Christian concept of music, the serious musical outlook of antiquity could not simply be discounted. It possessed in its tradition too great a worth for Christianity not to adapt it and to give it a Christian basis.

The history of Greek music was compiled by pseudo-Plutarch about A.D. 100. About the time when Christianity shouldered the task of furthering intellectual progress, writers like Martianus Capella (5th c.), Boethius (475–524), and Cassiodorus (490–580), produced a summary of ancient musical teaching on the basis of the writings of ancient musical theoreticians which they often understood but poorly. They represent, although frequently in a muddled fashion, the final summing up of ancient musical teaching and at the same time the beginnings of a metrical musical theory based on the ancients.

After the reorientation of Christian music in the fourth century, and the spread of Christianity among the "higher classes" who were trained in the ancient culture, whatever of ancient musical practice that could be made to serve the Christian spirit was adopted into Christian life with the necessary changes. Christian cult-music and ancient musical views had remained aloof from each other during the first few centuries, but a compromise was bound to follow. This was achieved by those Christians who had become acquainted with ancient music and its mathematical and metrical principles through their general training in ancient culture and to whom the chants used in Christian worship, oriental in origin, appeared as something quite novel.

This *rapprochement* between the ancient and the Christian is most noticeable in the writings of Augustine and in the changes in his musical outlook. The influence of Varro and the dominance of ancient metrical theories, as seen in the first five books of his *De musica*, stand in sharp contrast to the Christian reinterpretation that follows in the sixth book. The contrast of *ratio* (intellectual studies) and *auctoritas* (authority), which is used in the first books to set the limits between music and grammar, is recognized in the sixth as the domination of religious authority over all thinking. Hence he had to free himself from acknowledging exclusively the mathematical proportions in melody, harmony and word-tone unity which were the basis of ancient musical ideas, and to see in music a possibility for Christian prayer life and Christian expression. His approval of *canere in jubilatione,* the unfolding of pure, text-free melody, and his recognition of a metrically independent performance *secundum morem orientalium,* which is stressed especially in his later writings, were the novelty that Augustine, with all his roots in the ancient musical notions, formulated as the Christian musical view.

The idea that what a man cannot express in words he must tell God by means of pure melody, so that in prayer the music is an amplification of the text, shows the intrinsic deliverance of Augustine from the ancient view of music, even though externally he clings to the system of ancient musical theory. Thus the disengagement of the Christian musical view from the ancient gradually took place and with it the Christian adaptation of ancient musical theories, which were thus preserved. From the fourth century on, pagan scholars lost the lead to Christian thinkers, who handed on to future generations the intellectual heritage of antiquity, but only after sifting it and refurbishing it in Christian fashion. Thus, in the decline of ancient culture during the turmoil of the Migration of Nations, ancient musical theory survived as a positive force adopted by Christianity. An undercurrent of ancient thought continued into the Christian Middle Ages and, through the influence of outside forces, had its effects on medieval musical life.

LITURGY AND MUSIC

In contrast to the problem encountered by music in general, which had to be solved during the first Christian centuries by the gradual Christianization of life as a whole, the music of worship had to be considered immediately and intrinsically. A problem arose in the fourth and fifth centuries; namely, the precise relationship between liturgy and music in the divine service. This problem was the more acute because in the cultivation of music for worship not only ritual but esthetic values had to be acknowledged and weighed. This was the period when new forms of music were being developed for worship, and ancient musical theories were being taken in hand to give Christian musical life energy. Intellectual unity was already so far destroyed that common people had different interests in the pursuit of music than the more cultured who regarded music more as an art in the service of the Church than as a ritual form of prayer. Hence when Augustine, who had made an analysis of the musical theory of his time in his work *De musica*, relates in his *Confessions* that he "fluctuates between the peril of indulgence and the spiritual profit" to be found in the Church's singing, it is proof of the difficulties which the newly-introduced musical attitudes led to. The spiritual and religious aspect of music was the basis that had to be offered the Christian as the foundation of his musical ideas. This attitude was the reason why the secular music of the day, external in its direction, was so frequently rejected. Its power, which belonged to the *pompa diaboli*, had to be removed, according to Tertullian, Hilary, Ambrose, Augustine and Gaudentius, by the cultivation of psalms and hymns.

Thus in the fourth century Christianity shared two contrasting musical cultures, one local, ancient, metrical, and the other a traditional spiritual possession of the Christians of old, originating in the Orient and in Mediterranean culture. One was a musical view that looked inward (contemplation), the other one that looked outward (joy). These had to be amalgamated. We know little about the particular phases of this evolutionary process. But the result is well known; this was the arrangement of the church melodies by Gregory the Great (590–604). As a consequence, liturgical rigidity replaced spontaneous ritual, and musical tradition replaced patterned improvisation. In other words this is the victory of Western order over Eastern ecstatic meditation. Although these contrasts may not have been realized fully at the time, by recognizing the liturgical melodies as part of the realm of music, a start was made toward freeing liturgical music from ritualistic legalism. While still intimately attached to the liturgy, it would nevertheless be governed by the laws of musical language which would continue to be a great influence.

CHAPTER 2

Treasury of Liturgical Song

TRADITION AND PERFORMANCE OF ECCLESIASTICAL CHANT

The compilation of the Church's chant by Pope Gregory marks the first great impetus in the development of church music in the West. The fact that at the same time Isidore of Seville was concerned over the tradition of liturgical melodies and their careful preservation by memory-work (since there was as yet no system of notation) is a further proof of the new orientation of music and musical culture at this period. It is also an indication of the problem, now increased in importance, of preserving such a tradition. The founding of the *schola cantorum* grew out of this necessity.

Progress was made toward preserving the melodies by a system of notation, although the spirit of ritual music was quite alien to any accurate method of notation borrowed from the music of antiquity. However, the ancient notation was forgotten, not because it was unknown to Christians, but because they apparently had been unable to adapt it to their concept of cult music. A suitable method of indicating intervals within a given system was not rediscovered until many centuries after the standardization of the liturgical melodies, and then only after many unsuccessful attempts.

In Christian art the essential thing is not the individual musical note but the melodic formula linked with the cult; just as today it is the foundation of non-European cult music. In notation this melodic formula

17

had to be presented plainly. By a graphic representation of the melodic movement it had to form a visual prop for memory and tradition. The chironomy current in the Orient served as the basis for a system of notation that proved very useful in practice. Beginning with the marks for accentuation, reading and punctuation, it led to the formation of the neumes both among Italian Christians and among the Christians of the East.

Tradition continued to be the essential method of preserving the melodies, with the neumatic notation acting as a support. The musical laws for the composition of melodies in accordance with the notions of form led to the distinction between the "natural singer" or *cantor* and the *musicus*, who had studied these laws of musical theory. In the early Christian centuries such a distinction would have been strange, even though solo singing was used and recognized together with congregational singing. The soloist's task was not looked upon precisely as an artistic one but simply as a part of the musical ritual. An indication of the change in conception from the fourth century on, is the special artistic aptitude required of the cantor. And, as we learn from cemetery inscriptions, such artistic skill was recognized. Solo singing and choral singing became purely musical means of expression and so created the distinctive development of solo and choral forms which, under the differing musical circumstances, led to their respective independence.

Until the end of the third century the ecclesiastical language in Rome was Greek and the forms and chants of worship were borrowed preponderantly from the East. However, with the gradual adoption for worship, in the fourth century, of the language understood by the majority of the people, problems were created concerning the development of a Latin service free from secular and heretical influences. The Latin liturgies took various forms. The usages and chants found in Latin-speaking countries were shaped into various liturgies, the Roman, the Milanese (Ambrosian), the Gallican, and the Spanish (Mozarabic), with chants more or less different and distinct, although showing a common basis. Apparently the Roman liturgical chant developed more independently and departed more widely from the primitive Christian forms, because the most ancient customs and chants survived in the non-Roman liturgies. The melismatic richness found in the chants of these liturgies is an indication of this, because in non-European music generally the preponderance of melismatic passages is a mark of the older version. Differentiation within the liturgical practices of the West must have taken place in the fourth century, when the basic change from cult to liturgy began and with it the shift from a cult chant to a musical conception of song for worship.

WORD AND TONE IN CHURCH SONG

The evolution of church song in this epoch was determined first of all by a compromise in the word-tone problem. While ancient music had produced the closest association between text and music, with the rhythm of the word and its spoken accent linked to the music, the lesson (*lectio*) and psalmody of early Christendom introduced a new relationship between text and music. Its revolutionary novelty was in contrast to the ancient conception of the word-tone relationship. The basis was no longer speech accent, speech rhythm and speech melody which made use of a special melodic formula to correspond to each emotion (*ethos*); instead, there is a recitation on one tone, that is, a stylizing of the natural speech forms in favor of a purely musical phenomenon. Although the punctuation is definitely intertwined with the word and the structure of the sentence, it also becomes a purely musical stylizing, established in a formula. Stylizing and melodic formula both show the independence of the music, to which the text is subordinated.

LITURGICAL RECITATIVE

The simplest melodic formula is found in the liturgical recitative, used in versicles, lessons and orations to vary the stylized declamation on one note. The subtonal *tuba* or tenor (a,g,b) and the subsemitonal *tuba* (f,c,b flat), as well as the related placement of the whole and half-tones of the melodic formulas, offer an essential distinction for the songs and their expression.

1.	Pa - ter no - ster	qui	es in coe - lis
2.		Sanctificetur	no-men tu - um
3.		Adveniat	regnum tu - um
4. Fiat vo	lun - tas tu - a	sicut in coelo	et in ter - ra
5. Panem nostrum quo - ti - di - a - num		da	no - bis ho - di - e
6. Et dimitte nobis de - bi - ta no-stra		sicut et nos dimit- timus debito-	ri - bus no - stris
7. Et ne	nos in - du - cas	in ten- - -	ta - ti - o - nem.

Among the oldest Western orations is the Mozarabic *Pater noster*
whose formal structure becomes especially clear in the outline on p. 19.

PSALMODY

The most important form peculiar to Christian cult music is psalmody,
adopted by Italian Christians from the Eastern Christians who in turn
had adopted it from the treasury of oriental song. Psalms and canticles
are contained in the fifth-century *Codex Alexandrinus*, the oldest liturgical songbook. They were widely used at the vigil service as well as at
the celebration of the Sacrifice. Tertullian and Ambrose were especially
earnest in advising the singing of psalms which combine cult and music
in a prayer form. This type of song, in both its substance and its form, is
quite different from the heathen secular music, and thus least liable to the
danger (stressed by Clement of Alexandria) of being contaminated by
the worldly devices of chromatics and enharmonics. The oldest type of
psalm singing appears to be the solo performance, taken from the syna-
gogue practice, with the congregation answering either in a refrain or by
repeating each of the lines. This *cantus responsorius* is attested to for a
long period in both Italian and Spanish practice, especially as an addition to the readings. The psalms were sung to fixed melodic patterns
which fit the textual structure. The precentor interchanged various
formulas according to the text to be sung or the position of the song in
the ritual.

This link with the rite itself in the choice of the psalm melody and its
modification in performance kept the recitation of the psalms completely
free from every contrived musical practice along the lines of pagan art.
It was not till the fourth century, when the Christian ritual attitude was
replaced by the ancient esthetic conception of music, that artistic expression became a determining factor in the performance. Two different
methods of performance appeared, simple choral psalmody and freely
improvised solo psalmody. At the same time in the West the performance
was assigned to choirs of men and boys. This provided different possibilities for performance, namely, by soloist, choir of men, boys' choir,
or combined choir in octaves. This variety invited a certain musical evolution resulting in the creation of various forms for soloist. It had the richest
possibilities for melodic development. Other forms were arranged for
the choir and for the congregation, whose psalmody was simplified.

Through the interchange of various groups and the forms determined by them a musical enrichment of the divine service was achieved.

Psalm-tone for Choir, from the Office

Be - a - tus vir qui timet Do- mi -num in mandatis eius vo - let ni - mis

Psalm-tone for Choir, from the Mass

Qui ha - bi - tat in adiuto - ri - o Al - tis - si - mi

in pro - tec- tione Dei coe - li com - mo - ra - bi - tur

Solo Psalm-tone, from the Responsory (Maundy Thursday, 4th Response)

Bo - num _____ e - rat e - - i si na - tus non

fu - is set _____ ho - mo il _____ le _____

Solo Psalm-tone from the Tract (Third Sunday in Lent)

Ec - - ce si - - cut o - cu - li ser - vo _____

rum in ma - ni - bus Do - mi - no - - - rum

su - o - rum _____

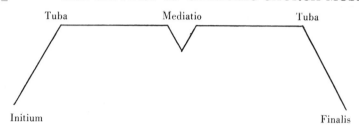

Basically, psalmody is a musical formula to which psalm verses, each different in structure, are fitted.

This diagram indicates a rigid organization, even though the melodic formulas for intonation, mediant, and final cadences bring a certain relief. The text, whether long or short, no matter what the contents of the individual verses, must be forced into this standard form used for each verse of all psalms. The unvarying melodic formula for dissimilar verses is the fundamental novelty that psalmody presented in contrast to ancient musical practice.

The subsequent development in the liturgical music of the Middle Ages, and in fact all vocal music of the following centuries, was the result of this freeing of the word from dependence on accentual rhythm together with its stylization beneath a purely musical melody. The method of reciting the epics of Nordic and Slavic peoples rests on the same principle of a melodic pattern, which has its own set of laws. These are seen especially in the limitation of tonal range and in the distribution of melodic centers. This method also admits of purely melodic amplification by embellishment without necessarily taking into account the words of the text. If the words are taken into account in certain instances it draws them away from subordination to the music and stylizing. Indicative of the importance of the music in psalmody is the fact that as a rule no account is taken of the words. The embellishment of this melody can depart from the tenor reciting note, modify the clauses, and in the case of solo psalmody create an art that begins with improvisation, but finds its chief assignment in the variation of the pattern, which variation in turn is regulated by formulas that are musically determined. Certain groups of formulas are used uniformly. Later the elaborations which originally were improvisatory and were continued by tradition, were written down and standardized. Thus many a formula improvised on again became stylized.

There is an account of how Ambrose, at the time of the persecution by the Empress Justina (386), instructed those who were loyal to him by antiphonal singing, a method already current in the Eastern Church. While the divine service of early Christianity was conducted with the least amount of external solemnity, with only an internal vitalizing of sacrificial intent, by the close of the fourth century there was a new outward evolution which presented music with special possibilities of development. The union of antiphon and psalm — with the antiphon originally repeated after every psalm verse — is already established in the Rule of St. Benedict (480–543). Here psalmody has been permitted a musical development, whereas the *cantus in directum*, as the opposite of this music-inspired attitude, originated as a continuation of the method of singing the psalm straight through, without antiphon or musical embellishment. The necessity of introducing this simple method of performing the psalms is found in the musical embellishment of other methods of performance, and therefore it was not emphasized until "musicality" had dominated the performance of the psalms. In the Benedictine Rule, in the writings of Caesarius and Aurelianus, and in the Ambrosian Breviary the *cantus directaneus* is expressly mentioned. *Cantus directaneus* and the musically developed performance of the psalms are opposites. This tendency to incorporate exclusively musical ideas is clearly a tendency away from a purely ritual attitude and could be masking a certain danger of secularization. Consequently it is understandable why Pambo, Abbot of the Monastery of Nistria in Egypt in the fourth century, should severely upbraid one of his monks who was inspired by the chant. But the idea that art, too, must serve to praise God kept such an ascetic attitude from becoming general, even though certain bounds had to be set to the musical development in the divine service. The establishment of liturgical forms and, in general, the working out of the liturgy and its meaning, as was done for Eastern Christianity by the monasteries of Syria and Egypt and in the West especially by St. Benedict and his disciples, offered the limits within which an artistic cultivation of chant was possible. As early as the second half of the fourth century Rome had a school for singers whose task it was to infuse liturgical concepts into art and thus encourage an artistic, liturgical chant practice in place of a freely improvised cult music.

Cassian approved lengthy melismatic chant for the Egyptian monasteries of the fourth century, and the Rules of St. Benedict, and of Paul and Stephen (6th c.) did the same for the West. The liturgical bond had so strongly determined the chant that the *Regula Pauli et Stephani* expressly stresses the point that the liturgical character of the individual chants may not be altered by free musical modification, and that the lesson and the melismatic chant especially must be used for their different functions in the liturgy.

ALLELUIA MELISMATA

Besides the melismatic rendition of solo psalmody, a purely melismatic art was introduced into Western church music by the Alleluia. Here, as Augustine asserted, the melody alone, without text or declamation, had special expressive value, so that the music by itself was treated as having as much expressive value as the liturgical text.

The recognition of this textless melismatic art, which was connected

Alleluia from an Ambrosian hymn

with psalm verse, was of fundamental importance for liturgical music in Western Christian worship.

HYMNS

The hymns stand in marked contrast to this purely melodic development. They incorporate a compromise between text and music and are to be regarded as a sort of free devotional literature of early Christendom alongside the fixed psalms. Because the heretics frequently availed themselves of this means, the Council of Laodicea (4th c.) ordained that only texts from Holy Writ be allowed to be used in the liturgy, but as with the psalms, the extreme ascetical position was not upheld. Instead efforts were made to sift the supply of hymns and the way they were performed, and then to incorporate them into the chant of worship as a free religious mode of expression. Through the efforts of Hilary of Poitiers (✝366), the hymn came into the West from Syria where Ephraem had cultivated it and from Greece where Gregory of Nazianzus had done the same. It was, however, Ambrose (✝397) who contributed to its spread and development. Thus, from the fourth century on, a further extension of the treasury of ritual music was found in the hymn, although a careful organization and scrutiny of the music for worship was necessary to avoid loading the service with pieces textually and musically unworthy.

In the beginning the melodies of the hymns were strictly linked with the ancient meters in a syllabic rhythm, but after adopting popular elements they developed in the West into free melodic creations, independent of the long and short values of prosody.

Hymn of St. Ambrose

Ae - ter - ne re - rum con - di - tor Noc-tem di - emque qui re - gis Et tem - po - rum dans tem-po - ra Ut al - le - ves fas - ti - di - um.

MELODIC STRUCTURE AND LITURGICAL LINK

In all Gregorian chants uniform melodic material is found, built upon basic formulas and variations, combined into a close unity of composision both in form and motif structure. The embellishing formulas are used in set groups but at the same time are linked to their liturgical position. There is a juncture here of a musical principle with a ritual one. Two texts can be identical as to wording, but they will have different meanings depending on the different places they occupy in the liturgy, and this difference in meaning will be made plain in the musical setting the text is given. From the fourth century on, the central position of the liturgy and its exposition in music are gradually but definitely asserted. The text was important, but the music gave it its liturgical significance and thus gained a new nexus. This is made clear in the various settings of the *De profundis* that follow, for these differ according to the liturgical use of the text, either as a choral or solo psalmody.

Alleluia-verse (23rd Sunday after Pentecost)

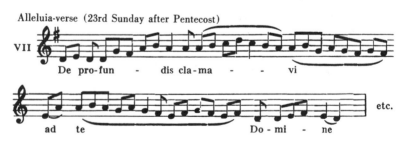

De pro - fun - dis cla - ma - vi ad te Do - mi - ne etc.

Tract (Septuagesima Sunday)

VIII — De pro-fun - - dis cla - ma - vi ad te Do - mi - ne

Offertory (23rd Sunday after Pentecost)

II — De pro - fun - - dis cla - ma - - vi ad te Do - mi - ne

Antiphon (Wednesday, at Vespers)

VIII — De pro - fun - dis cla - ma - vi ad te Do - mi - ne

Choir Psalm-tone

VIII — De pro - fundis ad te Do - mi - ne Domine exaudi vo - cem me - am

Choir Psalm-tone (Office of the Dead)

De pro-fun-dis ad te Domine Domine exaudi vocem me - am

MODES

The formulas were melodic phrases using a fixed relation between the whole and half steps, either on the reciting note or at the fifth. These were sometimes modified, showing how variation can be effective. These changes then brought into prominence certain melodic centers, but as the meaning of the formulas was gradually lost, the connection between these centers and the range of the melody led to the theoretical construction of the modes. Thus a new basis for musical interpretation was created especially in connection with the rational modal teaching of antiquity which here, as in the Middle Ages, had abandoned the teaching regarding *nomos* and *ethos*.

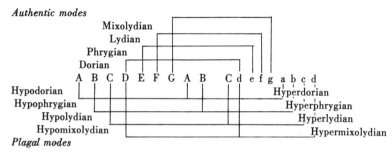

The distinction between hypo- and hyper-modes, which is based on the position of the formulas, soon disappeared, since by the octave transposition only the range was decisive in the system, and the mode was determined by the range and the chief tones. The uncertainty of the ♮ and ♭, which in the medieval system counted as one note, caused the latter's avoidance as a chief note in the system, in contrast to the natural order indicated above. The following arrangement of the modes was the result.

Mode	Range	Final	Tenor
I	d—d	d	a
II	a—a	d	f
III	e—e	e	c
IV	b—b	e	a
V	f—f	f	c
VI	c—c	f	a
VII	g—g	g	d
VIII	d—d	g	c

The progressive harmonic interpretation of these modes since the thirteenth century was given its final expression in the theoretical extension of the system by Glarean in the sixteenth century. Major and minor tonality changed the character of the old church modes.

After the eighth century this system of "church modes" coordinated all the liturgical chants, although some of them, having been shaped by other principles, lent themselves to this arrangement only with difficulty. This created an opening for centuries of theoretical analysis in the tonaries.

CHAPTER 3

The Gregorian Tradition

STANDARDIZATION OF THE ROMAN LITURGICAL CHANTS

While on the one hand, from the fourth century on, the very core of the problem of church music was the settlement to be made between it and the musical viewpoint of antiquity, on the other hand the spread of Christianity also involved a settlement with the racial peculiarities of the peoples that were being evangelized. At the same time, with this settlement and stabilization within the Church, there also arose the necessity of establishing the basic form of church music and thus guarding it against misinterpretation, as well as seeing to its proper transmission and spread. The central position of Rome, emphasized since the fifth century not only on a political but on a cultural basis, rendered this possible. Rome sought to substitute its own ecclesiastical chant and liturgy for the great variety of chants and liturgies to be found throughout the West.

After many diverse developments and adjustments from the fourth to the sixth centuries, the basic shape of the Roman liturgy and of its chant was finally achieved about the turn of the seventh century. In spite of contrary hypotheses advanced by Pierre Gussanville (1675), Georg von Eckhart (1729), or François August Gevaert (1890), it is usually conceded that this standardization of the Roman chant, so fundamental for all future musical development, can be attributed to Pope Gregory I (590–604). He recognized the importance of a consistent liturgical tradition for Rome's position in the Church's ecclesiastico-political life, and so he provided a uniform liturgical and musical recension of the forms of worship for the Church in the entire West during the Merovingian period. The Sacramentary was newly edited and designated at first for use in the stational services of Rome itself, while for the *Missae peculiares* (low masses) the old Gelasian Sacramentary continued in use. Later in Gaul a new revision of the Sacramentary was made with a view to fitting the liturgical forms originally intended for Rome itself to circumstances prevalent outside Rome. Likewise the Office and its chants, especially the psalms, were rearranged. The chants for the Mass and the Office were gathered from a rich store of melodies, and supplemented where necessary. Their rotation in a cento-antiphonary followed.

Liturgy and chant were molded into a unity in which everyone had his appointed tasks. In other words, the celebrant did not repeat what the choir sang; both had their special liturgical assignments. This was extremely important for the place of chant in the service and was the foundation for the intrinsic connection between liturgy and church music. Thus, in spite of its emancipation from a ritual attitude, and in spite of its basically artistic nature and development, music once more succeeded in combining with the liturgy in a unity of worship.

But in the development of the *Missa privata* in the period that followed, church singing lost this original liturgical function. From the moment that the priest recited the liturgical chants jointly with the choir and the liturgical task was completed by the spoken word alone, chant lost its unique liturgical value and instead acquired the character of a mere decoration. This presented it, however, with a fresh possibility for free artistic development. This inner readjustment of liturgy and church songs brought about slow changes that occurred at various periods in different locales. One important intermediate stage in this development is represented by the *Missale plenarium*, which included in one volume not only the priest's prayers and chants but also the choir's chants with their melodies; thus the duties of the choir were apparently absorbed by the priest. This custom, which persisted even down to the fifteenth century, shows how strongly tradition continued to operate.

Creating this tradition was the task of the *schola cantorum* which was newly established by Gregory I. The handing down of the liturgical chants rested in the main on instruction by ear; it was only later that written notation assumed importance. The *schola cantorum* promoted the correct handing down of the melodies and their artistic performance, which grew in importance with the new situation of liturgical music. At the same time, the *schola cantorum* also guarded the chants from change through free improvisation. They were now standardized and it was this standardized version which was to be preserved and spread. Although the centralization of the Church did not reach full development until the Carolingians, the *schola cantorum* was a great power in centralizing the inner ecclesiastical life and absorbing local forms rooted in popular tradition.

SPREAD OF ROMAN CHANT

About the time a compromise between the Christian and the ancient attitude toward music was reached in the standardization of liturgical music, the Western community was changed by the Migration of Nations and the advance of Germanic peoples into the crumbling Roman Empire. The Western empire, after the division of 395, finally ceased with the so-called "Fall" of Rome in 476. Numerous Germanic races moved toward Italy following the Germanic troops who had already replaced the old Roman armies. There was a mixing of races and this was of importance for the further development of liturgical chants. Vandals, Ostrogoths, Suevi, Burgundians, Franks and Alemanni settled down and contributed their talents to rekindle the spark of ancient culture, almost extinguished in these storms.

In musical life, as in other spheres, the church's leadership reached far beyond the merely ecclesiastical. The artistic promotion of music, even secular music, as well as its theoretical study, was in the hands of the clergy. Thus it was necessary to delineate clearly the limits of ecclesiastical and secular music. This was done under Pope Leo I and Pope Gelasius I in the fifth century and also by the Rule of St. Benedict in 530.

Originally intended only for Rome, the Gregorian version of the service melodies was made to assist the centralization which was being promoted in all spheres of society. Of course the introduction of this version met with some opposition in places that already had their own version of the melodies. As late as the ninth century the monastery of Monte Cassino was forced to abandon the Ambrosian chant at the bidding of the pope. In Milan, however, in spite of every pressure, the Ambrosian chant was retained and even as late as 1497, Pope Alexander VI had to confirm the Milanese rite. Thus even today in many places a liturgy and chant is followed that is older than the Roman, although in the course of years its range has been considerably restricted. This holds true, in a way, also of the Gallican liturgy. Unlike the Ambrosian rite the Gallican was not able to withstand the pressure of Pepin and the Emperor Charlemagne who introduced the Roman melodies, with the result that in many places the local forms were abandoned or else they were mixed with the forms of the Roman chants. In Spain, through the influence of the Goths, who followed a Greek-Byzantine musical tradition, a special church chant was formed. Its standardization under Isidore of Seville (560–636), along with an infiltration of Gallican chant, produced a liturgical and musical treasury that became predominant in Spain and southern France. Of capital importance for the formation of Spanish chant was the domination of the Moors, whence the name "Mozarabic" for the Spanish liturgy. This chant, which in the course of time grew more and more stylized, came into contact with an oriental practice which influenced it both in its formation and its performance. To avoid the ever-growing danger of falling back into a totally oriental musical attitude, a movement was started toward the end of the eighth century to shift the Spanish church chant to the Roman. In spite of the opposition of the people, the Spanish liturgy after a lengthy struggle succumbed to the attack that was led by circles which stressed European culture and by Rome, which sought to strengthen its central control by every means possible. But it was not until the eleventh century that Pope Gregory VII, with the support of King Alfonso of Castile, celebrated the victory of Roman chant on Spanish soil, although even to our own day some local points of Mozarabic liturgy have survived. Indeed, even where the Roman chant became dominant, vestiges of the ancient local liturgies were retained.

ADJUSTMENT OF ROMAN CHANT TO LOCAL MUSICAL CULTURES

The spread of the Roman ecclesiastical chant was faced by quite different problems where existing liturgies were not revised or supplanted but where the missionaries encountered entirely new conditions. In the time of Gregory I the Anglo-Saxons were made acquainted with the Roman chant by the missionaries who arrived in 516 under Abbot Augustine from whom they received the first copies of the Roman Antiphonary. Roman singers such as Jacobus, Paulinus, Hadrian and others, found apt pupils in the Anglo-Saxons, including Aeonan, Putta and Benedict Biscop, who handed on the Roman tradition. A direct contact with Roman practice was again established through the Roman archcantor, John, during the closing years of the seventh century, and in 747 the Council of Glasgow ordered that the ecclesiastical chant conform to the books sent from Rome. Thus a center of Roman chant was established in England that radiated to other countries, especially Germany, in connection with missionary work. An adjustment, however, had to be made in England not only with the local Anglo-Saxon musical tradition but also with the pre-Gregorian liturgy introduced by Roman troops, evidence of which is found in what is known as the *Sacramentarium Bonifacianum*. Elements of the pre-Gregorian musical practice continued to crop up and frequently necessitated a correction of the chants according to the Roman model.

The pre-Gregorian chant practice established in the Frankish kingdom by the *Imperium Romanum* was much stronger than that in England. For political reasons Pepin (752–768) and Charlemagne (768–814) insisted on the Roman chant. Bishop Chrodegang (742–760) created a center for the Roman style in his chant school at Metz, and Charlemagne erected his Schola Palatina at Aachen where the Roman chant was taught. Still the opposition of the people to the Roman chant was so great that Charlemagne was forced to give up his plan for a complete unity of church chant. Paul the Deacon (c. 790) and Alcuin were charged with the task of producing a version that would combine local peculiarities with the Roman type. Among other things the Introit psalm was shortened and the so-called "Romano-Frankish" version of the Office was created. This abbreviation is a special mark of the Western evolution of liturgical chants which eliminated the oriental tendency to amplify various forms. But this did not complete the standardization of the ecclesiastical chants in the Frankish kingdom. The Metz chant books were again altered at the start of the ninth century in accordance with an Antiphonary brought to Corbie by Abbot Wala. Amalar was commissioned by the emperor to fashion a new Frankish Antiphonary which, in spite of the argument of Agobard of Lyons in favor of the old forms of the Office, contained further abbreviations.

The new version of the liturgical melodies underwent many local changes, especially on German soil where, under Henry I (919–936) and Otto I (936–973) the formation of a German nation gradually took shape. The people gave the liturgical melodies their own particular forms. Local musical traditions created special versions, particularly in northern

Germany, where they survived until the nineteenth century in the chants of Trier, Cologne, Münster and Mainz. In southern Germany, where the Alemanni and Bavarians had been settling from the third to the sixth centuries, the new missionary effort encountered a Christian liturgy that reached back many years, planted there by Roman colonists. Combined with traditions of the new races it gained a form all its own in the vicinity of Passau. This locality was the scene of missionary activity more intensive than anywhere else, with influences that ranged from the Irish-Celtic culture to the Italian, Gallic and Spanish. The long survival of ancient Roman culture reinforced the local variations in the chant which often did not give way to any unification until the introduction of the Roman liturgy after the Council of Trent.

Considering this multiplicity of versions of the liturgical chant, the creation in this vicinity of a vital center for the Roman tradition was of capital importance in the endeavor to achieve unity. The task was undertaken by the Abbey of Reichenau and by a monastery which had, since the ninth century, surpassed all others in importance: St. Gall, where Roman, Irish-English, and Romano-Frankish elements of ecclesiastical chant were intermingled. Formerly it was thought that St. Gall was principally a center of chant creativity. Rather it served more to propagate the Roman chant and to absorb the various local traditions. The spread of the Roman chant, at a distance from the northern and southern centers, led to further adaptations because of local variants. Some of these were so strong, like the Alemannic version of the Swiss Benedictine congregation and various diocesan chants, that they have survived to the present.

The effect thus achieved within the body of liturgical chants, together with the special forms that developed, were the results of a musical viewpoint based on folk elements. On the other hand, the care of souls presented conditions, especially in German countries, that demanded a shortening and revamping of the liturgical melodies. These melodies had been developed in the services of the monastery, but the Germanic peoples, settling as they did in the farm lands, brought Christianity and divine worship out of the towns into the country. Unlike the monastic and episcopal churches, the country parish with its special problems of caring for families and its limited resources for externalizing divine worship, could adapt itself only with difficulty to the grand developments of the liturgy and its wealth of melodies. There had to be some adaptation or remodeling of the liturgical melodies, according to circumstances, usually in the form of dropping them or at least shortening them. Soon centers influential in reshaping the divine service sprang up in rural areas and from the eleventh and twelfth centuries onward the flourishing medieval municipalities produced conditions for the cultivation of church music which broke new ground in combination with popular song materials (processional songs) and music for festive solemnities (polyphony). The liturgical melody that had its development in the monastic and cathedral churches won a new position that had great influence on the future formation of the chant.

CHAPTER 4

New Forms

NEW FORMS AND REMODELINGS OF LITURGICAL CHANT

By the start of the second millenium the liturgical chant forms were essentially fixed in outline. But from the ninth century on new forms, developed from the popular piety of the communities in the new lands won for Christianity, were gradually added to the large store of liturgical chants with a view to bringing them in line with popular tastes. Something similar had already occurred in the East in the early Christian centuries, with hymns and songs appearing alongside the psalms as the expression of the native religious sentiment. The poetical creations of Venantius Fortunatus (c. 600), with their finely polished, classical handling of the Roman language (*Pange lingua* and *Vexilla regis*), are examples of this sort. In line with the Western rejection of the melisma, emphasis in the new forms was placed on syllabic settings, and predetermined melodic patterns were abandoned in favor of newly-composed melodies. As a result an entirely new interpretation of the whole store of traditional melodies was brought about, redirecting their further evolution until they were once again restored on a historical basis in the *Editio Vaticana*. The shortening or elimination of the melismata, as well as the reinterpretation of the melodies and the relocation of accents according to new principles of declamation and new melodic stresses, was the starting point for the appearance of many modified versions and new compositions.

TROPES

In the ninth century the basic form taken by these new efforts at chant composition was the trope. It was in this manner that Western musical thought made its deepest inroad into the liturgical melodies and developed new expressive forms of church music. The trope is a musical as well as a literary form, demonstrating anew the essential unity of liturgical music. It was aimed at revitalizing a liturgical chant that had grown rigid both in shape and in conception. A style of personal piety created a reinterpretation of standard texts. The melodies, however, were retained; that is to say, words were set to existing melodies, or else sections — both the text and the music — were appended. The first traces of this new art are found in southern France, and it received a special character at St. Gall where it was linked with the name of Tutilo. The art emerged in the sixth and seventh centuries with the standardization of the liturgy which then left no room for the free shaping of a personal style of devotion. The trope thus became the means of popular religious expression. Although the texts of the tropes represented an effort to revitalize the liturgy in all parts of the church year, the selection of music for the texts was determined by the intention of eliminating long melismatic passages, or if they were to be kept, of supplying them with a text. As a result, wordless but richly melismatic texts, like the Kyrie, lent themselves to troping ; e.g., *Kyrie clemens rector.*

Codex 383 from St. Gall

1. Cle - mens rec-tor ae - ter - ne pa - ter im - men - se
3. E - ter stel-li - fer no - ster no - stri be - ni - gnus

e - - lei - son Ky - ri - e
e - - lei - son

- - - - - - - lei - son. 2. No - stras nec

ne   vo - ces   ex - au - di   be - ne - di - cte   Do - mi - ne.

The Ite Missa est, too, was troped; e.g., *Ite* sine dolo et lite. Pax vobis-cum *Missa est; Deo* semper agite in corde gloriam et *gratias.* But other texts already supplied with many words were also troped, like the Gloria, the lessons, the texts of the Proper, the Office responsories, etc. For example at Christmas: *Gloria in excelsis Deo. Et in terra pax hominibus bonae voluntatis.* Pax sempiterna, Christus illuxit, gloria tibi, pater excelse. *Laudamus te.* Hymnum canentes hodie quem terris angeli funderunt Christo nascente. *Benedicimus te.* Natus est nobis hodie salvator in trinitate semper colendus. *Adoramus te.* Quem vagientem inter angusti antra praesepis angelorum coetus laudat exultans. *Glorificamus te,* etc.

If the melodies did not correspond to the interpolations in the text, the melody had to be extended. The next step was to compose a new melody. This was especially necessary when the trope took great liberties with the liturgical text and went beyond the mere bounds of interpolation, as, e.g., the trope for the Gloria of the Marian Mass:

Prague Codex, U.B. XIV H. 27

Do - mi - ne fi - li   u - ni - ge - ni - te   Je - su Chri - ste   spi - ri - tus

et al - me or - pha - no - rum pa - ra - cli - te   Do - mi - ne ...

In many instances the trope demanded a repetition of the melody, especially when it added a translation to the liturgical text, as in the following troped epistle:

Missal 520, Library of Chartres

Jocundi-tatem et exul-ta-ti-onem the-sau - ri - zavit su-per e - um

Joi - e san fin ioi - e   du - ra - ble ioi-e   ce - le - stre ioi-e establе...

SEQUENCE

The development of the sequence, or prose, follows the same lines as the development of the tropes. Here, too, was an effort to reshape melismatic sections by underlaying them with texts, but in contrast with the tropes which took in every sort of form, the sequences were attached to the *Alleluia jubilus*, thus forming a special class within the tropes. The sequence was also cultivated in a special way at St. Gall, where Notker Balbulus was chief practitioner, but its first development took place in southern France and Ireland. At first the sequence supplied a text for the *Alleluia jubilus (melodiae longissimae)*, turning it into syllabic chant. Soon this text was given poetic form, with an end rhyme on the sound *a* to correspond with the Alleluia. The multiplication of strophes led to the double strophe arrangement and the repetition of portions of the melody. Further development smoothed out the form into a symmetrical arrangement between strophes and pairs of strophes and in the relationship of melody and text.

Al - le - lu - ia

Christmas Sequence

Gra - tes nunc o - mnes red - da - mus Do - mi - no

Among the many sequences certain melodic types stood out as unifying forces and were even given special names. Thus the melodies *Eja turma, Concordia, Occidentana, Cithara*, etc., became the basic tunes for hundreds of sequence texts. From the eleventh century on, rhyme and hymnlike rhythms predominated in the sequence. Adam of St. Victor (✠1192) is the most important composer during the later development of the sequence, which was extraordinarily widespread and offered a way to ornament the festivals of local saints. Thus the sequences were important supports of provincial and national art, which continued to manifest these peculiarities. The various collections of sequences differ in their arrangement; the French prosaries begin with the Advent sequence *Salus aeterna,* while the German texts put the Christmas sequence *Grates nunc omnes* at the beginning. The revision of the *Missale Romanum* ordered by the Council of Trent left only five sequences: *Victimae Paschali* by Wipo (✠ c. 1050), *Veni Sancte Spiritus*, probably by Stephen Langton, Archbishop of Canterbury (✠1228), *Lauda Sion* composed by Thomas of Aquin in 1263, and *Dies Irae*, mistakenly attributed to Thomas of Celano (✠ c. 1255). The *Stabat Mater*, a hymn ascribed to Jacopone da Todi (✠1306) but perhaps by St. Bonaventure (✠1274) or John Peckham (✠1292), was inserted in the missal as a sequence by Pope Benedict XIII in 1727 when he extended the feast of our Lady of Sorrows to the universal Church. So from the rich store of sequences written during the Middle Ages only a few from the late period of their development are in general use today.

CANTIO

Because the sequences were especially fitted to be vehicles for expressing personal piety, they were suited for use outside the divine service and so grew independent both in form and content until, like the tropes, they evolved into a new form for the personal expression of religious thought. This new form was called *cantio*. *Cantiones* were really spiritual songs which, in their melodic shape, stemmed from musical experiences that were popular in origin.

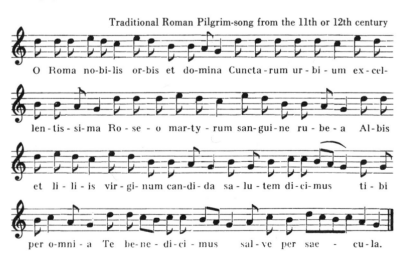

Traditional Roman Pilgrim-song from the 11th or 12th century

O Roma no-bi-lis or-bis et do-mina Cuncta-rum ur - bi - um ex - cel-

len - tis - si- ma Ro - se - o mar-ty - rum san-gui-ne ru - be - a Al-bis

et li - li- is vir- gi- num can-di- da sa - lu - tem di-ci-mus ti - bi

per o-mni - a Te be-ne - di-ci - mus sal - ve per sae - cu - la.

RHYMED OFFICE

There is still another way in which a shaping of free forms stemmed from the liturgy. The rhymed office, which gradually became more and more prominent after the tenth century, at first merely employed meter and rhythm, but from the eleventh and twelfth centuries on it emphasized rhyme. In Julian of Speyer (✠ c. 1250), who created unprecedented models of this in his offices of St. Francis and St. Anthony, and in John Peckham, whose Office of the Blessed Trinity was widely used, the rhymed office attained its high-point as a musical type. In the rhymed office the basic ideas of the liturgy were indeed preserved, but at the same time a fundamentally new form was created, crowded with new ideas. Rhymed offices were quite widespread until the sixteenth century, but were almost entirely suppressed by the Tridentine reform. Only the Franciscan and Dominican Breviaries retain this art at the present time.

Invitatory, from the Office of St. Francis, Matins

Re - gi que fe - - cit o - pe - ra, Christo con-fi- te -an - tur cu - jus in san - cto vul-ne -ra Fran - cis - co re - no - van-tur.

HYMNS IN THE VERNACULAR

By means of the trope, sequence, *cantio* and rhymed office, personal piety achieved outward expression in connection with liturgical chants. But the ever-growing departure from the liturgical chants, which were the starting points, led to further forms, especially when the vernacular began to be used as an aid in understanding the chanted Latin. Insertions in the vernacular were made in the tropes. To be noted in particular, the *Kyrie eleison* from the Litany of the Saints was made into an acclamation and, at least in German lands, used outside the liturgy and expanded by means of vernacular texts from the eighth century on. An account from Prague in the tenth century makes mention of the singing of "Christe kinado Kyrie eleison unde die heiligen alle helfant uns Kyrie eleison." In a hymn from Freising in honor of St. Peter we have the first evidence of a German vernacular hymn from the ninth century. This popular art was promoted in connection with the spread of pastoral work in the country and also in connection with ecclesiastical folk customs. Gerloh of Reichersberg in 1148 says that "the whole world celebrates the praises of the Savior with songs in the vernacular; this is true especially among the Germans." Along with independent creations in the vernacular there were translations of tropes and sequences and hymns so that the forms of these chants and their melodies became German hymns. There was the freely-composed *leis*, which got its name from the troping of the *Kyrie eleison*. And then the adoption of the sequence form in the German hymn led to the *leich*, which had a changing melody for each pair of metrically dissimilar strophes. Among the earliest examples of the art is the *leich*, "Ave vil liehtir meres sterne," which imitates the Sequence, "Ave praeclara maris stella."

These songs clearly betrayed their Latin models and generally borrowed the melody of the chant they were built on. But at the same time there was a development of vernacular hymns that were freely composed both in text and melody. The singing art of the trouvères, troubadours, and minnesingers included sacred songs as well as secular. And during the period of the crusades the ideal of knightly poesy brought about an enrichment of ecclesiastical hymnody in the vernacular. Strophe and rhyme presented the outward form that determined the melodic shape. Just as courtly and popular secular songs developed their own forms, so also the church hymns. Special development occurred in pilgrim and processional songs, in hymns for the church year (Christmas and Easter carols) and in hymns honoring the saints.

The penitential hymns developed into the flagellant hymns of the fourteenth century. The melodic structure, clearly arranged and joined to the text, and the anticipation of the major-minor tonality, are suggestive of popular German art which developed similar forms for folk song and dance.

Hugo v. Reutlingen 1349

Ma - ri - a muo-ter rei-nû maît Erbarm dich û - ber die cri - sten-hait

Erbarm dich û - ber di - nû kint dî noch in die-sem el - lind sint.

As a result of the separation of the German hymn from its basis in the liturgical chant a new development occurred and presented the hymn with many various characters and uses during the course of the fourteenth century.

A determining factor in the development of the church hymn in the vernacular was the effort to promote an understanding of the liturgical action by means of popular presentation. The textual materials were taken from the conceptual world of the common people, and from the thirteenth century on, the melodies assumed more and more the character of popular musical language. This tended to dramatize liturgical things, and thus to further the understanding of the liturgy all the more.

RELIGIOUS DRAMA

The dramatic division of the trope into dialogue, as we find it in the tenth-century trope from St. Martial in Limoges, led to the dramatic presentations especially at the Easter and Christmas celebrations, first within the confines of the liturgy and later independently. By the eleventh century these dramas had spread everywhere. In the Easter festival the women and the angel hold a dialogue like the following: *Mariae*: Quis revolvit nobis lapidem ab ostio monumenti? *Angelus*: Quem quaeritis . . . Germanic cult plays were not without their influence in developing this dramatic presentation. Later the "women's scene" was dramatized in dialogue; likewise the appearance of Christ to Mary Magdalen. Other scenes from the Bible also lent themselves to dramatic performance. And from the twelfth century on vernacular texts were introduced, making the plays more and more like folk plays. In the same way the dramatic production of the Christmas mysteries was developed — evolving into the plays of the Shepherds, the Magi and Rachel. Besides, there were musico-dramatic presentations not connected with the church year, such as the *Sponsus* play of the twelfth century (The Foolish Virgins), the Daniel play, the St. Nicholas play and others that were completely new creations both in text and music. In the *Ordo virtutum* of St. Hildegard of Bingen (✝1179) the mystery play achieved a certain magnificence which was shown especially in the distinctly national character of the melodies.

From the Ordo virtutem (Epilogue)

In - de tu - o re - gi - na hu - mi - li - tas

tu - o me - di - ca - mi - ne ad - iu - va me.

As the strict liturgical art that grew out of the trope developed independent literary and musical forms in the field of vernacular song, the religious play developed in the same fashion. The quest for popular appeal led to the development of a musico-literary form. The deepening of Christian conceptions among the people made an understanding of the liturgy necessary and for this purpose the new forms of ecclesiastical music served as means. Through the reforms of Cluny and Gregory VII (1073–1085), a stricter view of ecclesiastical thought was opposed to the secularism of the time, culminating in scholasticism in the area of science and philosophy, and in the great development of popular piety during the twelfth and thirteenth centuries. Here were incentives for a new evolution of church art, which on the one hand was an expression of those popular religious concepts that led to a mysticism most distinctively expressed in the German hymn, and on the other hand was an enhancement of the solemnities of divine service, brought about by a development of liturgical forms of song. Just as in Gothic church architecture the massive unities of Romanesque art expanded into a variety of motions and yet, from a higher viewpoint, organized these movements into a still greater unity; so music, too, was forced to form, out of the simple melodic line, an expanded mode of expression more consonant with the new artistic reform.

CHAPTER 5

Tonal Expansion

FIRST TRACES OF POLYPHONY

The new forms of the trope appearing in the ninth century signalized a
break in the old Gregorian tradition and became a starting point not only
for new monodic creations but also for polyphony. Here we have not only
the most vigorous breakthrough in medieval musical culture but the basis
for further musical development. In contrast to the arrangement found
in the current forms of the trope, where the troping is *juxtaposed* to the
liturgical text, we now have an arrangement where the troping is *superposed*. Various efforts to release the liturgical chant from its simple foundation and to achieve a new tonal form and purely musical development
began after the end of the first millenium to turn this vertical troping
into a substantial fundament for polyphony and for Western musical art
in general. The liturgical text and the liturgical melody continued to be
the core of the composition; the offshoot voices were an ornamentation of
a subjective kind which, in some forms, attempted a textual interpretation as in the ordinary trope forms, but from the musical standpoint endeavored to gain an independent tonal effect.

This brought about a new evaluation of music in the divine service.
Some forms were accounted a liturgical minimum, namely the usual Gregorian chants; and some were considered an enhancement of the solemnity but they lost, in the course of development, that deeper connection
with the liturgy. Thus polyphony, in spite of its link to the liturgical
chant in the *cantus-firmus* technique, attained a purely musical inter-

pretation and development only as late as the fifteenth and sixteenth centuries.

Even in the periods when the Gregorian chants were being standardized an effort was made to establish tonal vigor as a contrast to the melodic rigidity of the chant. The harmonic structure was created by a fusion of tones and so a simple broadening of the melody was formed by the use of paralleled fourths and fifths. The paraphonist of the *Ordo Romanus* in the seventh century (in spite of the objections brought against Peter Wagner's thesis by Amédée Gastoué and after him by Otto Ursprung) appears to have had the task of providing this tonal broadening of the melodic texture. The manner of performing the parallel organum was then presented scientifically in the *Musica enchiriadis* of the ninth century.

Tu pa - tris sem - pi - ter - nus es fi - li - us

It was the Nordic concept of music that created and promoted the standardization of tonal degrees and polyphony.

Besides the tonal broadening of the liturgical melody by means of strictly parallel voice leading in the blended intervals of octave, fifth and fourth, we find the use of contrary motion and a freer form that interchanged the motions.

Rex coe - li do - mi - ne ma - ris un - di - so - ni

Finally there was the free oblique movement over a bourdonlike held note, the so-called "rambling organum" (descant).

Organum of the 12th century (Vatican Codex Ott. 3025)

O - - - - - - - -

- - pe - - - - - -

ri - - - - - bus

Tonality and setting were the new media of expression added to the melody, with the latter no longer regarded in its purely melodic structure. In connection with the change in shape of church buildings from basilica to Gothic cathedral, the tonal problem for church music became ever more acute. Even though the use of the organ was still quite restricted, its introduction into the church was closely linked with the problem of tone and space. The great development of organ building in the medieval monasteries would hardly have occurred if the instrument had not won great importance. When Constantine Copronymus in 757 presented Pepin with an organ and this instrument was subsequently improved in the West, tone became the center of interest. In the same way the tonal problem became more important for the composition as a whole. The tone-broadening unity of the melodic line became the driving force in the new forms, already anticipated in the heterophony of antiquity. In the forms which Scotus Erigena cites from the writings of the Hucbald circle, the liturgical melody is undisturbed by this tonal extension, even when the organ was used for the held notes. The organ was styled a church instrument by Walafrid Strabo (✝849) and others, and Pope John VIII ordered one from Anno, bishop of Freising, in 873.

The accentuation of the individual note in the melodic line was the result of the emphasis on syllabics in the evolution of Western chant, and of musical theory since the eighth century. The establishment of set degrees within a series, which was the natural accompaniment of such a development, made possible a further movement of the voices and ended in making the voices independent on their parallel, oblique and contrary motion. This combination of various attempts at polyphony was represented in Guido of Arezzo (✝ c. 1050), John Cotton (11th c.), Aribo Scholasticus, the Milanese Anonymus and others. In these there is a gradual effort to move from a harmonic link of the voices with the *cantus firmus* to independence of the individual voices. Thus there de-

veloped in these *dupla*, *tripla* and *quadrupla* of the eleventh and twelfth
centuries a need for rhythmic independence of the voices, which led from
the practice of improvisation to the formation of a mensural theory and
its notation. This development was combined with the various efforts at
vertical troping and thus evolved the multitextual motet.

COMBINATION AND FREEDOM OF VOICES

In the Winchester Troper and in the eleventh-century manuscripts from
Fleury and Chartres the tonal extension was in the main simply directed
to, and bound up with, the *cantus firmus*. The independence of voices,
however, was promoted more extensively at the turn of the eleventh-
twelfth centuries in the sphere of the school of St. Martial in Limoges.
Thus the development of a polyphonic art with independent voices was
begun and a foundation laid for the whole subsequent Western evolution
of vertical composition.

The earliest solution of the problem of rhythm was the rather stiff
scheme of modal rhythms which were closely molded to the liturgical
melody and gave it tonal extension.

But gradually rhythm gained independence by the development of
mensural notation.

The organa of the Notre Dame school of Paris, whose chief masters
were Leoninus the *optimus organista*, and Perotinus the *optimus dis-
cantista*, illustrate a new attitude toward the liturgical melody.

Now the center of interest no longer lay in the Gregorian *cantus firmus*
but instead in the newly formed composition itself. The Gregorian *cantus
firmus* was indeed retained but it no longer determined the composition;
instead it was adapted to the setting and thus lost its character as melodic
lead. The emphasis on each individual note (already developed with the

Perotinus, Organum quadruplum: Sederunt principes

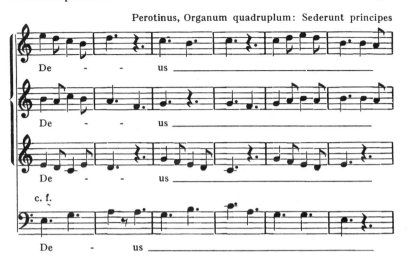

standardization of the chants) fitted in with these efforts and permitted the contrapuntal voices to interweave around a lengthened series of notes instead of an unbroken melody. These contrapuntal voices formed an independent composition by themselves. In such a setting the chant becomes an alien element. It was lifeless and could not yet be freed by the more lively types of motion allowed to the contrapuntal voices, like variation, figuration, hocket and the like.

It was therefore only a small step to discontinue the *cantus firmus* altogether and to invent all the voices. But the relationship of organal music to the liturgy made such a step impossible at first. Therefore this art, like the independent forms of horizontal troping — *cantiones*, songs in the vernacular and such — had its first development outside the narrower limits of liturgical music. Processional songs, introductory songs, and festive songs were created in free forms as *conductus*. Thus the second stage of polyphonic development was established. Even to our own day compositions linked to the chant and those not so linked stand side by side. And in its development the strictly liturgical forms were soon included, no longer, however, as a form of ecclesiastical music, but as a method of musical creativity of the Parisian Ars Antiqua type.

The *conductus* was the first independent form of polyphony to break both with liturgical melody itself and with the principle of the trope. Therefore the *conductus*, unlike the vertical trope, no longer had a multiplicity of texts. And the purity of free composition was guaranteed by the lack of any Gregorian *cantus firmus*.

12th to 13th century (Gastoué)

Ro - raut coe - li nu - bes

plu - - - unt stil - lant mon - tes

ARS ANTIQUA

The chant-linked organum and the free *conductus* continued side by side until the beginnings of the motet in the middle of the thirteenth century. In the motet a new art developed which combined the principles of both these forms. Besides France and Spain, England also contributed numerous works in the new combination. The Notre Dame school continued as the center of the new art.

In the motet we have the creation of a purely musical form of polyphony, striving more or less to be free from any liturgical link. From the various forms employed by the Parisian master Perotinus, who developed the composition from a simple *duplum* to a complicated *quadruplum*, a "motet style" was evolved for festive church music.

In the clausulas — little two-part sections and formulas — he presented general church-music practice with a form that quickly spread and developed. This art is handed down to us in the *Magnus liber organi*, which undoubtedly amplified and extended the technique of Leoninus' organal composition. While in the older organum the voices were linked to each other, the motet liberated them entirely from one another and consciously preserved their opposition. The motet became the greatest musical form of the twelfth to the fourteenth centuries. The mixture of liturgical and secular texts robbed it of its strict ecclesiastical character.

Triplum

I - po - cri - te pseu - do - pon - ti - fi - ces

Motetus

O   quam   san - cta quam be-

Tenor

Et   gau -   -   -

ec - cle - si - ae di - ri car - ni - fi - ces

ni - gna   ful - get

[debit]

Textually and musically the motet is simply a vertical troping of the *cantus firmus*. Texts in the vernacular and *contrafacta* were added to the *cantus firmus* in the same manner as interpretative liturgical texts. This kind of polyphonic performance, where each voice was given a special text, was at first incorporated in the Mass chiefly for parts of the Gradual and Alleluia, and in the Office for parts of the responsories. The clausulas of Perotinus were the basis for this development, which became a wide-spread species with many a melodic addition. The French motet, because it took the lead, stamped its particular character on the Latin. In the motets of the Montpellier Codex the end of the first important stage of development is indicated by a transition from rigid modal rhythm to a free mensural type, and by a reshaping of the square notation into mensural notation, especially because of the early work of Petrus de Cruce (c. 1250).

In the second half of the thirteenth century the motet was revamped in its entire structure. The melisma was included where formerly the modally syllabic voice predominated, and unity with the tenor, both as to text and melodic leading, was sought. The art of Perotinus flowed into the style of Petrus de Cruce. Johannes de Garlandia, Franco at Cologne and Paris, Jerome of Moravia, as well as later writers like Walter Odington and Johannes de Grocheo handed on the theory of the new art. It was developed in England as well as in France and continued to flourish along with the old modal and organal formations, till the fifteenth century.

II Music for Worship

CHAPTER 6

Regulation and Restriction of Church Music

DISPUTE REGARDING POLYPHONY IN THE CHURCH

Basic to the development of music was the recently achieved compositional technique of polyphony, with its many possibilities for expression. Using the same techniques of composition, secular and ecclesiastical music went their different ways, though often enough their paths met. Consequently, marking the limits between secular and ecclesiastical music became a problem, and the problem became all the greater as the development of secular music grew in importance. Even where the voices were grouped contrapuntally around a Gregorian *cantus firmus*, the secular elements had become the mainstay of the structure. The original aim of polyphony as a tonal decoration and troping interpretation of the *cantus firmus* was lost. So it came about in the twelfth and thirteenth centuries that numerous voices were raised to recall church music to an awareness of basic principles. They even called for a rejection of the newly acquired melodic forms. John of Salisbury (✝1180), Ælred (✝1166), Durandus (✝1296) and Roger Bacon (✝1292) complained about the new art and its mode of performance. Moreover Pope John XXII, in 1324, emphasized the central position of the liturgical melodies. The pope believed that the ancient polyphony, being a harmonic ornamentation of the Gregorian melody, represented a legitimate enhancement of the solemnity of the liturgical melodies on feast days. But the new art had stifled the Gregorian *cantus firmus* and thus estranged itself even from the liturgical link that helped to make polyphony ecclesiastical music.

POSITION OF THE CHURCH

Hence the polyphonic art which had been continually developing since the eleventh century became for the first time the object of a papal decree. The notion that the solemnity of the liturgy could be heightened by musical art and that the ancient liturgical melody did not represent the highest embodiment of liturgical expression was novel. So polyphonic music acquired the basis not only for its development, but for its limitation; it was to serve to heighten the liturgical melody and not go its own way autocratically. However, the border between being linked to the liturgical melody and freely shaping the melody along the lines of a progressive development of the techniques of composition led to difficulties in establishing a true ecclesiastical style down through the years to our own time.

The fluctuation of position toward a static liturgy and a living musical practice has, through the centuries, done as much to bring the problem of an ecclesiastical style to the fore as have the changes, local and temporal, of the technique of composition. The problem arose partly because the Church was no longer the sole leader in musical matters and was forced to take a stand with regard to artistic expression that had grown and continued to grow outside her spiritual sphere. In the decree of John XXII we find an attempt to solve the problem by rejecting any means of musical composition which expressed contemporary secular art, and which therefore would for the most part be an extremist foray into experimental techniques. New means of composition would be acceptable only after they had been tried and had lost their force in contemporary secular music; only then could they be used to create an ecclesiastical music that was universal, not given to extremes and free from echoes of secular music. This was to be the viewpoint of the Church for centuries.

The novelties to be found in the church music of the thirteenth century almost forced a move in this direction, toward a music estranged from contemporary art. Yet this historicism and conservatism did not produce a paralysis of church art, as the succeeding history of church music proves. The basis for the attitude expressed by John XXII was not the techniques of the period nor the movements in art, but rather the intellectual foundation of the artistic movements and their relationship to the Church. Therefore in the course of history, ecclesiastical polyphony has stiffened into a mere backward-looking formalism only during those periods when the religious attitude lost its power to create its own means of composition and to give materials at hand ecclesiastical significance.

The path of church composition was erratic until the period of the new ecclesiastical polyphony which, with its form and shape refurbished, became, like the Gregorian reform a thousand years previously, a new model of church music; and, even though in the very moment of its highest achievement it bore the seed of inner disintegration and subversion, it had a lasting influence on the development of the church music that was to follow.

TRADITION AND THE STYLE OF A PERIOD

Since the ninth century, personal piety had been seeking an outlet through music in worship. The shaping of musical experience at divine service has in every era tended to be dissatisfied with any restriction of the stylistic resources of any given period. As a result, all during the evolution of church music that followed, two tendencies were continually at odds and working against each other: the one attitude, conservative, linked to the liturgy and reactionary regarding stylistic resources, the other progressive, perceiving the personalized contemporary style as the ideal of church music.

CHAPTER 7

Conservative Forms

GREGORIAN CHANT

The principal support of tradition in church music was Gregorian chant. But the new forms that had developed on its foundation since the tenth century clearly showed that the chant was no longer valued, as in earlier years, for what it was. That awesome reverence for its tradition had disappeared and it had begun to be treated with utter freedom in line with the times. Several factors conspired to bring this about. The conception of the melody as so many individual notes, a conception given expression both in the disintegration of the melody in polyphony, as well as in the development of notation and of the theoretical and practical re-evaluation of the melodies — all this was bound to have an effect on the ancient melodies themselves, reworking them according to the contemporary conception. Moreover, differences in time and place had a part in the interpretation of the liturgical melodies, so that a great diversity is found even in the melodies themselves. National musical conceptions had erupted everywhere; consequently the process of change in the liturgical melodies which had already started at the time of their spread in the seventh and eight centuries, was given new impetus.

REVISIONS OF THE GREGORIAN MELODIES

Because of this multiplicity of versions of one and the same melody, it became impossible for people from different regions to sing together.

This was most disturbing to the religious orders, because their general chapters brought together monks from many countries. As a remedy, the orders felt it necessary to make regulations to unify the chants for general use within their own ranks. But all such efforts served only to point up the difficulty and actually brought in their train new problems. For one thing, the compromises themselves represented further additions to the already existing multiplicity of Gregorian versions. The Cistercian General Chapter in 1134, for example, ordered the simplification and unification of the liturgical chants. Repetitions of the text and new forms, like the tropes and sequences, were rejected; in the belief that a liturgical chant should move only within a scale of ten notes, the range of a tenth was strictly enforced. The effort to obtain a clearer tonality, furthermore, forced many changes in the melodic center, cadence, endings, etc. The greater part of this reform of the Cistercian chant was carried on by Guy of Cherlieu.

Communio Dom. III Quadr.

Pas - ser in - ve - nit si - bi do - mum et tur - tur

ni - dum u - bi re - po - nat pul - los su - os

In a similar manner the Dominican General Chapter entrusted to a commission the preparation of a unified Dominican version, but since the commission was composed of a German, a Frenchman, an Englishman and a Lombard, the great differences in national versions barred any unified result. It was not until 1254, with the work of Humbert de Romans, that any unifying regulation was actually passed; the attempted solution was based on the Parisian chants. The work was completed in 1267. Unlike the Cistercian reform, the Dominican retained the melismas. The formulas for the lessons, however, were made subsemitonic.

These Gregorian reforms by the religious orders naturally included changes in the old melodies called for by contemporary developments. However, at the same time, because the basis was now one of established uniformity, the reforms safeguarded the melodies against any further shifts and remodeling that might be dictated by those local or temporal movements that in other instances affected the medieval liturgical chants and finally altered them absolutely. It was not until the age of printing in the fifteenth century that any considerable unification again gained ground. But by that time it was generally neither artistic nor liturgical interests that attempted to obtain the spread of a particular version; rather it was the interests of a publishing house. Even though unification of the liturgical melodies was important for a homogeneous celebration of the service throughout the Church as a whole, it nevertheless suppressed living and popular versions — local versions, naturally — in favor of a stiff conformity.

PERFORMANCE OF THE CHANT

Along with the transformation in melodic shape of the liturgical chants went a transformation in the manner of performance. This new concept of the Gregorian melodies that comes most clearly to view in polyphony (isolated note, lengthening of tempo, shortening of melismas, and the like) entailed in the performance of the liturgical melodies themselves a stressing of isolated notes and the consequent rupture of the melodic line, a lengthening of the tempo, shortening of the melismas and shifting of the melodic center.

Once polyphony had secured its independent development and its detachment from the liturgical *cantus firmus*, the liturgical melodies were sometimes employed in ancient organal fashion as a liturgical polyphony. In some areas such a way of singing survived right down to the sixteenth century, to a period when music had already achieved an entirely new development. This manner of singing was traditionally retained, especially for the lessons.

15th century Evangelium pulchrum (Breslau)

Au-di-e - bant verbum il - - li-us

The arrangement of voices given here is also found in faux-bourdon, with a similar manner of performance, especially in the hymns. The third-sixth harmony, fitted isorhythmically to the *cantus firmus*, continues the old tonal expansion of parallel organum in a newer harmonic interpretation. Lionel Power and pseudo-Chilston, as also Gulielmus Monachus, about 1450, report on this practice, mostly a form of improvisation, which presented an extension of the Gregorian melody by means of harmonic expansion without involving what John XXII had forbidden, the disturbance of the liturgical melody. Like parallel organum, faux-bourdon was produced by a strict parallel movement of all the voices.

G. Dufay, Kyrie de Apostolis

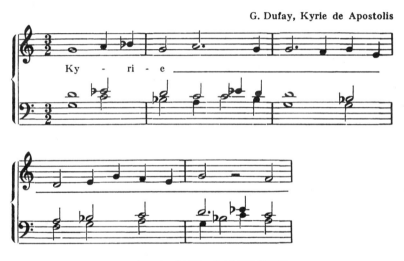

HYMNS AND CANTICLES

Melodies that had been expanded from the liturgical chants by popular devotion were now further enhanced by harmonic expansion, achieved through the use of every form of parallel movement. The *cantiones* and vernacular hymns, the *cantigas* in Spain, the *cantiques* in France, the *laudi* in Italy and the German *lieder*, all adopted in the fourteenth century a simple, parallel voice-leading in a quite conservative ecclesiastical style, and they retained this form, at least in part, even in the sixteenth century. The rich store of fervent songs that sprang up in the spirit of St. Francis of Assisi (✝1226), the *laudi*, had their first great development before the beginning of the fifteenth century.

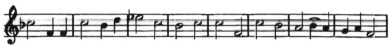

Glo-ria in cie - lo e pace 'n ter-ra Nat 'è l'no-stro sal-va - to - re

Thus for individual forms a useful style was evolved which was retained even during the later polyphonic evolution. This led to the formation of melodies characteristic of homophonic music in contrast to melodies of a more complex structure used in polyphony. However, during the ascendancy of the Netherlandic composers the two styles were conjoined, and continued to reappear together in various forms later.

CHAPTER 8

Origin and Development of Polyphony

ARS NOVA

The divorce of the new multivoiced church music from any connection with the Gregorian chant resulted in a setting aside of the Gregorian *cantus firmus*. This was actually a shift of emphasis from the *cantus firmus* to the contrapuntal voices. The mannerisms of hocket and the clausulas, against which John XXII had taken a stand, demonstrate the placing of emphasis on contrapuntal voice-leading and tonal effect. In secular music, these developed and evolved quite independently.

Hocket in a 14th century Gloria (Ms. Apt.)

The melodic, rhythmic and harmonic novelties thus formed made even deeper inroads into church music. These features were stamped into the works of Philippe de Vitry (*c.* 1290–1361) and Guillaume de Machaut (✝1377), and were theoretically explained by Jean de Muris (c. 1290– c. 1351) and his school. About 1320, Philippe de Vitry gave this artistic school the name Ars Nova, contrasting it in his treatise with the older motet and the survivals of the organum style in ecclesiastical service music. Novelties appeared in every sphere of melody. Rhythm sought to create new possibilities of movement by its *tempus perfectum* and *imperfectum*, that is, by its triple and duple time and its divisions of the unit. This new art achieved form in the motets of the *Roman de Fauvel*.

Roman de Fauvel

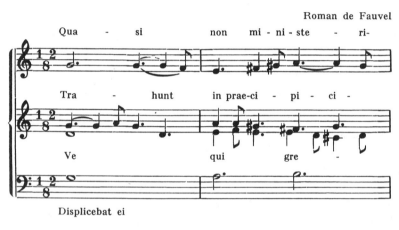

The rhythm of the old motet was suppressed, and tonality was at the same time broadened by means of semitones. Similarly the combination of two contrapuntal voices working together in rhythm and harmony shifted the stress to these elements themselves and displaced the *cantus firmus* — often arbitrarily distributed according to the demands of the setting — from its leading role in the motet. The effort to achieve a unity in the whole setting led to tying the various voices together by means of imitation, diminution and augmentation, with the *canon* providing the strongest link. The upper voice, which had taken the lead in the ballad, was also given a more emphatic role in the motet, especially in descant paraphrasing. Instruments furthered the harmonization. In this art the organ gained new tasks.

THE POLYPHONIC ORDINARIUM MISSAE

This art, now no longer bound by the liturgical melody, took new strides also in the choice of texts to be set. Besides polyphonic settings of the Proper there was also the polyphonic Ordinary and in the course of musical development this eventually took the lead.

For musical reasons emphasis was put on texts which actually have a subordinate place in the liturgy, and so at divine service the musical stress was shifted. The first cyclic mass composition was the *Mass of Tournay* (14th c.) ; the sections with fewer words are written in a three part *conductus* setting; the Gloria and Credo employ the Gregorian melodies in an elaborated form.

Gloria from the Mass of Tournay

Do - mi - ne   De - us   À-gnus De - i

On the other hand the Mass of Machaut, the greatest master of the new art, supposedly written for the coronation of Charles V in 1364, uses just the opposite technique. The sections with fewer words use the Gregorian melodies, while the Gloria and Credo are set in a *conductus* style. Thus, even in the fourteenth century, the link with the Gregorian chant was no longer considered essential, and this freedom became a musico-structural principle. Similarly in these early mass compositions another principle became established, namely, the use of a melismatic form for the sections with shorter text and the tendency to use a syllabic form for the more extended texts. In the course of the development of the mass, this principle continued as the rule.

G. de Machaut

e - ley - -

e - ley - son

e - - ley - - son

e - leyson

- - - - - - - - - son

Besides these two cyclical masses there were also many polyphonic settings of parts of the ordinary. Surprisingly, the settings of the Sanctus, Benedictus and Agnus Dei, being a continuation of the priest's chants, are relatively less numerous. So, in spite of musical novelties, there was still a widespread feeling for the proper position of music in worship.

FRENCH AND ITALIAN MASTERS

Machaut discovered in the secular ballade the best outlet for his innovations in melodic setting and form. In the same way he introduced new devices in motet composition. For example, instead of continuing the borrowed melody in the tenor part throughout, he wrote freely for the various voices. He employed the isorhythmic technique without consideration of the difference of texts used in the *motetus* and the *triplum*.

Machaut

France was the center of the new art. Avignon's position as the residence of the popes until 1377 gave it considerable importance musically. And in the fourteenth and fifteenth centuries the art radiated out to Spain and northern Italy, at the same time manifesting closer links with the secular ballade. Italy, in turn, became a new center of the art, and certain features of the Italian art, like the smoothing out of the melodic setting and the rhythmic and melodic equalization in form and harmony, took the lead in the further development of the Ars Nova.

About 1340, the peculiar Italian form of the new style was given a definite stamp in the work of Giovanni da Cascia and Jacopo da Bologna. The new art was displayed in the secular forms of the *caccia* and the madrigal, while church music, still quite conservative and tradition-

Ghirardello

bound, at first manifested a certain caution. But in the musical circles of Florence and northern Italy the new forms of expression were soon employed in church music as well, in ever increasing frequency. Until the work of Johannes Ciconia the influences of the older French forms (*motetus, conductus*) and of faux-bourdon continued to determine the search for newer expression.

The great number of possibilities that could be adopted in the renewal of church-music styles, especially forms and devices of secular origin, led to distinctive fashions and forms in several leading centers. In Rome, it was not until Pope Martin V (1417–1430) that the new art gained any significant leadership. Marchettus of Padua and Prosdocimus de Beldemandis sought to give the new art a theoretical foundation and evaluation.

The emphasis on music gave an impetus to textless musical composition for church and created the first important development in organ music in the works of Francesco Landino (c. 1325–1397), Antonio Squarcialupi (✠ c. 1475) and others.

DEVELOPMENT IN ENGLAND AND THE NETHERLANDS

Thus in Italy and France about the beginning of the fifteenth century there was a gradual movement to emancipate the composition tonally and rhythmically from the rigidity of the isorhythmic patterns. At the same time the contrapuntal voices, although independent in movement, manifested a closer bond with the Gregorian melodies. This development was especially noticeable in England and in the Netherlands. In Germany service music made only restricted use of the new devices, even in the fourteenth and fifteenth centuries, and to some extent an organal *cantus firmus* technique was preserved even as late as the sixteenth century. England, too, clung to the Gregorian melody as the dominant factor in the ecclesiastical composition, but made an effort to get away from forms employing parallel motion like the organum, gymel and faux-bourdon, without letting the freedom of movement do away with the link to the chant. By paraphrasing the chant melody and by fitting the *cantus firmus* into the setting, reshaping it both melodically and rhythmically, a new technique of handling the *cantus firmus* was adopted similar to that of Guillaume Dufay and Gilles Binchois. Thus the Gregorian melody continued to form the skeleton of the composition of which it was an integral part. The problem of the polyphonic composition and its relation to the chant reached a new stage. The descant took the lead, and the melody radiated from it in a free development.

Gloria from Mass IX

Dunstable, Gloria (Codex V, Trent)

The theoretician Johannes Tinctoris (c. 1446–1511) rightly acknowledged England as the source of this new art of his time. The Englishman John Dunstable (c. 1370–1453) was the leader of this movement. In

Burgundy and in the Netherlands this new English art fused with the older techniques of composition that had evolved on the continent. The leading light in the Burgundian group was Gilles Binchois (✝1460); in the Netherlands, Guillaume Dufay (c. 1400–1474).

The upper voice took on a prominence which led to a readjustment of the role of the lower parts. Although at first the lower voices did not share in the complete design in an equal degree with the upper voice, they were now put on a par with it. Efforts were made to find devices to unify a composition. Voice pairing led to an equal treatment of all parts. Unification was further achieved by repetition of thematic material and by reuse of forms. The various parts of a cyclical mass, for example, were linked by a unifying theme. When the Gregorian chant was no longer prominent in the new composition, a new device of placing the simple performance of chant melodies alongside polyphonic choruses was introduced, and the choral intonation was used to usher in the Gregorian melody that could no longer be clearly heard in the course of the polyphonic composition.

The old use of two voices in duet was preserved in four-part writing by pairing various voices, sometimes in strict canon, and also by such contrapuntal devices as the crab-canon, the mirror-canon, diminution and augmentation. Other techniques of contrapuntal writing, together with changes of time signature, modulation and the practice of writing for four voices, brought great complexity to the art.

These devices have been called the "arts" of the Netherlanders, but they were not mere tricks of composition; they were a serious attempt to obtain a unity in the work, in contrast to the older disjunction between *cantus firmus* and the other voices.

In the descant mass and motet, the *cantus firmus*, borrowed from Gregorian chant, is found not in the tenor part, but in the upper voice, where it is frequently disguised by figurations. The tenor *cantus firmus* was derived from the chant or from secular or religious songs, while the other voices obtained their melodic material as far as possible from the *cantus firmus*. Johannes Grocheo and the seventh book of the *Speculum musicae* emphasize the arrangement of these freely-composed parts drawn from the *cantus firmus* (*color, talea*) together with their vertical relationship (*consonantia, concordantia*).

The *cantus firmus* has been shifted to the top voice as the thematic material.

Apart from the Old Hall manuscript and a few other music manuscripts,

Mass VIII

Ky - ri - e

G. Binchois (Codex V, Trent)

the Trent Codices are the most important source for the early evolution of this art. Although practiced widely, its development differed in various countries. By and large, in spite of various details of style, the trend was everywhere in the same direction. With all the voices of equal importance, the *cantus firmus* could appear freely in all of them. Balance and movement were achieved in the various parts by use of melismatic passages, the proper use of dissonance and consonance, an avoidance of stiff mannerisms and attention to the humanistic interpretation of words by declamation. By means of through-imitation (*durchimitieren* [1]) a solution to the problem of the closed melody was achieved. Thus the unity of the vocal setting was also accomplished, replacing the disjunction between instrumental and vocal lines in the Ars Nova.

[1] A term coined by Hugo Karl Riemann to designate the application of imitation equally to all the parts, so that the melodic lead moves from voice to voice. [Trans. note.]

Instruments were joined to the vocal setting *colla parte*, that is, they played along with the voices. Voices and instruments were separated only when the instruments substituted for missing parts. The use of instruments rested not on structural expansion of the composition, but on its tonal expansion. Just as at the start of the second millenium polyphony was regarded as an enhancement of the chant performance, so now the *colla parte* use of instruments was considered an enhancement of polyphony. It therefore was employed especially at the service on solemn feast days. The structural mixture of instrumental and vocal sound as found in the Ars Nova period was thus overcome.

The tonal concentration that ensued had its counterpart in the harmony. The vertical expansion demanded alterations by means of accidentals (*musica falsa* and *musica ficta*).

THROUGH-IMITATION

The search for a new style led to through-imitation, which acquired certain definite forms in the work of Johannes Ockeghem and Jacob Obrecht and their circle. The unity of composition that was sought was realized in the canon. In his *Missa cujusvis toni* Ockeghem (c. 1430–1495) pursued the abstraction of the contrapuntal composition to a point where the same melody could be sung in various modes by different placement of the clef and key signatures. Thus the last step toward an objectively constructed art in church music was reached, as is shown in Ockeghem's thirty-six-voiced *Deo gratias* with its four nine-voiced canons.

etc.

But important though such steps were in the achievement of contrapuntal technique, the most important accomplishment of this so-called "Second Netherlands School" was the imitation of the initial motif in phrases taken up by each of the voices in turn. This successive or through-imitation, modeled on the canon but with some paraphrasing, was the foundation for the further development of polyphony, as well as the later evolution of the fugue and the through-composed technique. This device promoted textual clarity by presenting those portions of the text that belonged together in a musically complete form separated from other portions.

PERSONAL EXPRESSION

This treatment of the text, in contrast to the art of Ockeghem with its concentration on musical structure, was utilized especially by Jacob Obrecht (c. 1450–1505). For his technique he drew on his mystical, yet objective, sense of liturgy, which he fused with a vital, yet subjective, form of expression. His clear composition technique was founded on this background, but it likewise embodied popular influence which shaped his themes as well as his rhythmic and harmonic style. An imaginative personal interpretation of the liturgical text led him to a free and expressive use of his melodic material. The Gregorian *cantus firmus* was employed thematically in every voice and incorporated, often with variations, in the shaping of the composition.

In this way a personal mode of expression returned to church music, leading eventually, after further developments, to aberrations such as those that had brought about the decree of John XXII at the beginning of the fourteenth century. Antoine Busnois, Johannes Regis, and others pursued similar attempts at technical progress along the lines laid down by Ockeghem and Obrecht.

Josquin des Prés sought to bridge the gap between these two positions. He spiritualized the technique which in Ockeghem occupied a middle ground, and added to it a verbal expressiveness. This effort to attain expressiveness also facilitated the adoption of devices from secular music, especially the chanson, where progress had been made in obtaining that new ideal of declamation in grammatical accentuation and musical expression. Of importance in judging the ecclesiastical propriety of Josquin's church music is the stylistic contrast between his chanson com-

Pe - trus A - po - sto - lus et Pau - lus Doc - tor gen - ti - um

ip - si nos do - cu - e - runt ____ le - gem tu - am Do - mi - ne.

Obrecht, Mass on "Petrus Apostolus"

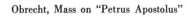

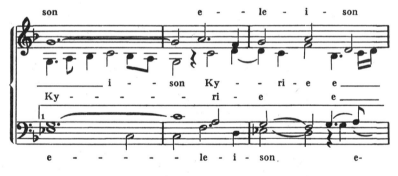

positions, with their rather free style, and the restraint manifested in the shaping of his ecclesiastical works, especially in the stylistic refinement of his masses. Correspondence in theme and melodic structure, as well as in the sequences of imitation and the combinations of voices, tended to advance a style intent on clarity. In Josquin's church music the humanistic conception of words and the Renaissance notion of symmetry make their appearance. Thus a homophony in straightforward declamation, aimed at basic expression, found a place in the general contrapuntal plan; and four-part writing took the place of the older three-part style.

Josquin, Missa Pange lingua

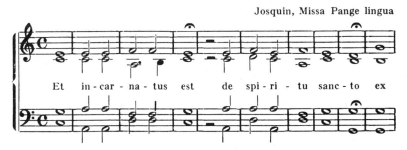

Ma - ri - a vir - gi - ne et ho - mo fac - tus est.

Like Josquin, other pupils of Ockeghem — Loyset Compère, Antoine Brumel, Johannes Verbonnet, Pierre de la Rue — all endeavored to achieve this combination of structural clarity and verbal expression. They developed a style embodying mystical refinement with personal expressiveness. Others, too, including Alexander Agricola (1446–1506), Gaspar van Weerbecke (✠ c. 1514), Antoine de Fevin (1473–1515), and Jean Mouton (✠1522), evolved a style of composition embodying expressiveness. In this way homophony as a structural technique based on the text attained a prominent place in composition alongside strict contrapuntal progression.

A new era had dawned and had shaped its own artistic expression. The universal culture of the Christian West, which had reached a crest in the thirteenth century, was being reassessed by a new subjective type of thinking. At the same time an inner corruption of ecclesiastical life can be detected. Life and thought were dominated by a veritable fanaticism in both good and evil. Mysticism and popular piety developed a more vulgar form, and encroached on ecclesiastical life. In these circles a new form of artistic expression developed, important both for the Church and for secular music. It first appeared among the Netherland masters in the North. The secularization of ecclesiastical life forced personal consciousness into so deep a subjective experience of religion that the new artistic expression was led to establish new musical forms for worship. Herein lay the great strength of the Netherland masters, who sought to develop in their art a medium of worship, but always at the risk of losing contact with popular musical experience because of their self-conscious concentration and self-centered spiritualization.

SERVICE MUSIC FOR THE CHURCH

There must have been a profound reason why, in contrast to the grandeur. of ecclesiastical art, the composition of *laudi*, hymns, and service music retained definitely simple forms, even if these had to be unearthed from centuries-old traditions. In manuscripts of the fifteenth and sixteenth centuries in many regions a style based on organum appeared frequently along with simple faux-bourdon settings, either alone or coupled with more developed contrapuntal forms. This shows that the ordinary service music for church could reach no compromise with the complicated style developed by the Netherlanders. Indications of this tendency are the simple hymn setting, given new shape and adopted by the Lutheran service as its chief form, and also the widespread interest in medieval liturgical melodies with attempts at their simplification. It was only in their use of homophonic devices that the Netherlanders found themselves in line once more with the efforts and demands of service music in general. It thus appeared that there might develop an art generally appreciated and accepted that could become the basis for re-evaluating and revamping the position of technical innovations in church music.

Homophony, Polyphony and Polychoral Writing

VERBAL REPRESENTATION AND INTERPRETATION

The structural and technical advancement of music by the Netherlanders of the fifteenth century was conditioned somewhat by the renewed prominence given to the text.

The presentation of the grammatical word in declamation, its accent and the syntax of the phrase accorded with the desires of the humanists. In the odes set to music by Tritemius, Ludwig Senfl, Paulus von Hofhaimer and others, with their ancient meters, the device of declamation was used in the upper voice even though musical phrases were separated. In homophonic forms this shaping of the composition in accordance with the words created a musico-textual art of expression which developed a medium with musical depth by employing the lower voices in a role subordinate to the voice declaiming the text. This undermined the equality of the voices in the polyphonic composition, and led to a subordination of the lower voices to the upper voice, increasing the latter's power of expression. But it took a hundred years for the ultimate consequences to be drawn from these premises and for monody to become a new foundation for further musical development.

The personal and subjective interpretation of the text by means of the melodic structure and setting offered certain difficulties to the liturgical use of music, for a new attitude was formed toward the liturgical text. A personal and subjective interpretation instead of a mystical, objective adorning of the text by the music characterized this tendency, which

80

unfolded during the sixteenth century. This technique existed together with a more objective tendency in church music and soon sought its own place in church-music composition. However, its first full development was not in liturgical music but in extraliturgical song. The *laudi spirituali, madrigali spirituali,* religious motets and *cantiones* were shaped in this fashion, offering a way for a personalized style of expression. Both in secular homophonic forms and in religious music, harmonic media and tonality were expanded to produce new metrical forms.

This development in the sixteenth century of a religious art outside the sphere of strictly liturgical music was of great importance as a stimulus for a new style of expression. On the one hand it served as a link with the innovations being introduced in the madrigals, especially in Italy and England. On the other hand it proved to be a wedge for the introduction of new media into the strict ecclesiastical style. This more personal art gained entrance first in the music of the Office, in the psalms, hymns and vesper antiphons, but the composition of masses was much more reserved. It was only by very slow degrees that any of these innovations were admitted into the composition of the Propers.

The *Choralis Constantinus* of Heinrich Isaak (c. 1450–1517) was the first complete polyphonic setting of the texts of the Proper of the Mass for the entire church year. It was commissioned in 1508 and published in 1550 and 1555. Although structurally linked to the Gregorian *cantus firmus,* it frequently attempts an expressive style of composition, as is shown in the various settings that employ the same Gregorian melodies as the basis for the composition. From the Gregorian melodies the various themes are developed.

Verse of the Introit for the Mass of the Holy Ghost by H. Isaak

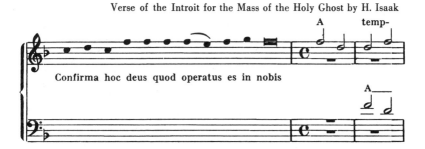

Symmetrical shaping of form and structure were quite obvious in his
contrapuntal settings. This manner of treatment was perfected among a
group of German composers of the second half of the fifteenth century,
and further developed by Heinrich Finck (c. 1450–1527), Thomas
Stoltzer (c. 1480–1526), and others.

Protestantism found the basis for its service in the simple setting of the upper voice. The chorale setting and the setting of psalms, especially in Calvinist circles (Huguenot psalms), made use of a simple structural form and so was quite similar to Lutheran church music. Because of Luther's insistence on the instructional value of congregational worship, with its national and popular associations, music was given a new task, different from its function in Catholic worship. As a result music, as an expression of such a concept, had to discover a new and different mode of development.

POLYPHONY AND THE OBJECTIVE CONSTRUCTION OF THE TEXT

The core of the development of Catholic liturgical music lay in the objective presentation of the text. Polyphony offered a means of doing this, which made it possible to present the individual word clearly but at the same time to avoid a subjective interpretation of the text because of polyphony's harmonic structure and rhythm. Thus a new ideal of liturgical art was created. Like the Gregorian chant of the Middle Ages, it was an expression of liturgical worship which employed new devices within a generally traditional style. The variety of creative materials which polyphony had at hand complicated this evolution. Already in the works of Ockeghem, balance in the composition was perfected to the point that further development lay only in the direction of a more lively expressiveness. Obrecht and Josquin des Prés were less concerned with new devices for achieving unity and balance than they were with enlarging the expressiveness of their music. This involved the greater use of the homophonic style, which was already predominant in extra-liturgical religious music.

The problem of the creative artist working in church music in the sixteenth century was not to choose between polyphony and homophony as such, but rather to establish the precise place of music in divine worship. Each of the styles had its own powers of interpretation. The use of both styles, together with an ever-increasing tendency toward tonality, marked the evolution of church music in the sixteenth century. While for Ockeghem the intertwining of voices in every contrivable way served to unify the composition, in later development it was the horizontal-vertical relationship that became the chief problem. The devices of canon and thorough-imitation succeeded in distributing the *cantus firmus* through every voice, but this horizontal balance was achieved at the neglect of the vertical relationship between the parts. A true balance in both respects was necessary to avoid shifting the centers of gravitation. Imitation at the fifth was the first step toward harmonic feeling in the contrapuntal setting, and the intonation of the melody in successive voices in imitation led to the clustering of tones and so to the establishment of a feeling of tonality for the whole composition.

NEW ART OF EXPRESSION

These new stylistic devices that appeared as early as the start of the sixteenth century were enhanced and utilized during the generation of Josquin's pupils. Nevertheless their purpose was not to achieve a more objective presentation of the text but rather a better interpretation of the text, together with compositional balance. For the musician the highest ideal was *musica reservata*, an art marked by a form of declamation and shaping of phrase typical of the Renaissance yet free from naturalistic tendencies. Andrien Petit Coclicus mentions as masters of this art, which was enhanced by the improvisation of the singers, Josquin, Isaak, Pierre de la Rue (✠1518), Brumel, and among the representatives of the younger generation, Ludwig Senfl (1492–1555), Cristobal Morales, Nicholas Gombert, Thomas Crecquillon (✠1557), Adrien Willaert, Clemens non Papa (Jacob Clement) and others.

Improvisation in performance included not only changes in dynamics (*esclamazione*), but also the structural alteration of the melodic line. In the North especially the practice of diminution was taken for granted in the performance of ancient polyphonic works, whether vocal or instrumental. For various movements certain definite variations were established. Thus, for example, according to Andrien Petit Coclicus, 1552:

Or, according to Hermann Finck:

Originally of purely structural significance, this system of diminution was soon coupled with definite efforts to obtain expressiveness and
was thus associated with the expressional style of the *musica reservata*.
The consequent obscuring of the text, however, eventually led to the
abandonment of this manner of performance. There was moreover some
hesitancy on the part of the Church about obscuring the text with the
music. Practically, however, this usage, so widely propagated, could not
be easily put down, but persisted all through the sixteenth century. It
took new life in the expressive coloratura of monody in the modern
sense. Among others, Lodovico Zacconi in his *Prattica di musica* (1592
and 1622) and Domenico Pietro Cerone in *El Melopeo* (1613) presented theoretical treatments of this art of diminution.

EXPANSION OF TONAL VALUES

The art of diminution had a way of contributing some of its tonal
charm to every style of writing, whether it was the strict polyphonic
work in the manner of Ockeghem, which cultivated thorough-imitation
and the *cantus firmus* or the thematically and structurally restrained
church composition (e.g., the parody-masses), or even the *reservata* art,
so free in its construction. Along with this sort of tonal emphasis we
find an interest in sound as such, demonstrated by concern over the
arrangement of voices and especially in the use of several choirs.

In polychoral art the emphasis on sound was pushed to such lengths
that for its sake even the polyphonic structure was sacrificed, and so
homophony assumed importance on a new basis. The greatest early
development of this polychoral technique was accomplished by Adrien
Willaert (c. 1490–1562), a Netherlander who had emigrated to Venice.
Other Venetian composers continued it, but the Roman composers of the
late sixteenth century utilized it even more. In alternating the singing
of the verses of the psalms between two choirs, the liturgical office
provided the external basis for the *cori spezzati*. In Willaert's *Psalms*

(1550) they acquired their distinctive form. Thus declamation and homophonic composition assumed new importance; new interest was given to the horizontal, linear setting by greater use of vertical harmony. This was determined by the desire for tonal expansion. Since the increased expressiveness of the music followed upon the multiplication of tonal effects, polychoral techniques naturally developed, as well as the practice of combining vocal and instrumental choirs. In addition there was a broadening of the harmonic palette by the use of accidentals. These strengthened the mobile traits of the harmony and at the same time gave added direction to the harmony of the cadences. This harmonic movement, which had its inception with Willaert and which was further developed by Cyprian de Rore (1516–1565), and Andrea and Giovanni Gabrieli (1510–1586; 1557–1612), was given its theoretical statement by Nicolo Vicentino (1511–1572). In the last years of the sixteenth century it began to embrace ever-widening circles, even though Gioseffe Zarlino (1517–1590) and others still emphasized the ancient ecclesiastical modal system and Henricus Glareanus (Heinrich Nores, 1488–1563), in his *Dodekachordon* (1547), added four new modes to the traditional eight, thus giving names (Aeolian, Ionian) to the modes which became our major and minor.

PARODY COMPOSITION

New expressive values were thus created, offering church music possibilities for personal expression that derived from the structural objectivity of the liturgical text but ended in a subjective enhancement of it. Music triumphed over the text. In line with this not only were the musical media increased but without scruple melodies and settings were made the basis for church compositions, even though the original texts with which they were associated had nothing at all to do with the church and were often, in fact, quite profane. Just as the music was made independent of the texts it had originally served (e.g., "O Rosa bella," "Malheur me bat," "Entre vous filles de quinze ans," "Je ne mange point porc"), so in the parody-masses it became independent of the liturgical text; it was church music that followed its own structural shape with its own musical expression. This completely destroyed the inner tie between music and the liturgical text which had still been preserved by the use of Gregorian themes, and opened the way to a purely musical development of the text. Although work artistically valuable and important could be produced, there was danger of forsaking the liturgical mission of church music and making music an end in itself. Consequently it was precisely these parody-masses that the reawakened liturgical sense of the second half of the sixteenth century attacked most vigorously, not only because of the original texts but because of the independence of the music from the liturgical text. To avoid the attack, masses which were based on profane models no longer cited the name of the model, but were called simply "Sine nomine."

SPREAD OF POLYPHONIC MUSIC

The development of the art of printing music made possible an even greater spread of church music. Besides the large folio-size choir book around which the singers could group themselves, the part-book appeared allowing each singer to have his copy. Octavio Petrucci (1466–1539) was the forerunner in the printing of polyphonic works by means of movable type. The new church music was disseminated everywhere — by Pierre Atteignant in Paris, by Tylman Susato in Antwerp, by Antonio Gardano in Venice, etc.

Printing disseminated the new musical devices throughout Europe, although local development continued. The Germans expanded their predilection for artistic structure; the French, their skills in rhythm and declamation; and the Italians, their techniques for harmonization and melody. The widespread use of art forms which were the expression of a particular national or racial attitude led to manifold artistic readjustments wherever native forces were at work. But on the other hand creative activity in church music saw a dulling of native emotions brought about by a striving to follow contemporary fashions and by centralized ecclesiastical laws, especially those which developed after the Council of Trent.

ORGAN PLAYING

The organ and organ music achieved an independent position in divine worship. Since the fifteenth century portative and positive organs were used not only to accompany the vocal setting but also for performance of independent preludes, interludes, and postludes. This organ music was linked thematically with Gregorian chant or endeavored to adapt itself to worship in free contrapuntal work. The notation for this art is the organ tablature. Organ composition livened the vocal structure, from which it sprang, by coloration. Arnold Schlick (1512), Hans Kotter (1513), Leonhard Kleber (1520–1524) and the organists of the early sixteenth century developed this art of coloration to a point where the coloratura itself and later the instrumental themes that evolved from it were employed as a basis for further compositions. Paulus von Hofhaimer (also known as Messer Paola, 1495–1537) was the greatest master of the art of the organ in the early sixteenth century.

P. Hofhaimer, Salve Regina

In the numerous organ tablatures of Nikolaus Amerback (1571, 1575, 1583), Johann Rühling (1583) and Johann Woltz (1617) there are many organ works based on Gregorian themes, as well as freely composed preludes which continued to win an increasingly broader place in organ music for the church. By the seventeenth century this had led to the development of the fugue. The Netherlanders and the North Germans influenced by Jan Pieter Sweelinck (1562–1621) promoted the development of the fugue and the choral prelude, especially for the Protestant service. The Venetians Claudio Merulo (1533–1604), Girolamo Cavazzoni (1542), and Girolamo Frescobaldi (1583–1643) developed an independent ecclesiastical organ music grounded partly in Gregorian chant, partly in free forms like the *canzone, toccata, fantasia,*

ricercare, passacaglia, etc. In Spain, church music for organ was developed especially by Antonio de Cabezon (1510–1566).

Like vocal music, organ music strove to achieve a more important position. It enveloped the songs that were constantly winning a larger place in worship and were actually pushing aside both the liturgical action itself and the liturgical melodies of the chant. Significant in this regard are the multivoiced responses which became quite widespread and replaced the chant responses.

Herpol

Ha - be-mus   ad   Do - minum   Di - gnum   et   iu - stum   est

Thus the continuation of the priest's chant, originally sung by the people according to a liturgical melody, was taken over by the choir which, in broadening its part in worship, continued to maneuver for an ever-richer musical share in the service.

CHAPTER 10

The Ideal Style of Ecclesiastical
Polyphony

ECCLESIASTICAL POLYPHONY IN ENGLAND, FRANCE, AND GERMANY

From the many streams of activity in church music during the sixteenth century an ideal style gradually emerged which endeavored to serve the basic liturgical attitude by means of polyphonic forms. Although echoes of liturgical melodies helped to strengthen the liturgical fitness of these polyphonic settings, what was essential was to be found in the objective arrangement of the musical composition, present even when a secular theme was used as the basis for the setting.

In England, as a continuation of the tradition of Dunstable which was developed further in the Netherlands, an ecclesiastical polyphony emerged that emphasized the alliance between text and music. By using simple themes related to the text, and by a contrapuntal equality of the voices, the English achieved an arrangement of both the harmonic-vertical and the contrapuntal-horizontal structure. English church music, with Robert Fairfax (1470–1521), John Taverner (c. 1495–1545), John Sheppard (✠ c. 1563), and others, manifested early in the sixteenth century a stylistic arrangement that was not then to be found in Italy or other European countries. Latin church music in the strict style was cultivated also by musicians of the Anglican Church. Christopher Tye (✠1572), Thomas Tallis (✠1585) and especially his pupil, William Byrd (1543–1623), who remained faithful to his Catholic belief, created polyphonic compositions in the more balanced style. Byrd's masses, motets, psalms and *cantiones* show him to be a master both of contrapuntal voice weaving and of objective expression. This adjustment between word and music found no similar stylistic arrangement in either France or Germany.

In the ecclesiastical creations of Clément Jannequin (✝ c. 1560), Pierre Certon (✝1572), Andreas Pevernage (1543–1591) and the many

Byrd, Credo

other French masters of the sixteenth century, a taut form of art that served to outline the text is found. As in the chanson, It lay In the direction of pure declamatory expression. In the Netherlands-Germany area, the mysticism of contrapuntal exaggeration continued to have an influence. Nikolaus Gombert (1520–c. 1552), Ludwig Senfl, Benedikt Appenzeller, Jakob Vaet (✠1567), Jacobus Clemens non Papa (c. 1500–c. 1558), and others display a contrapuntal intensity, paired with a folklike expression of melody. The structure lost its leading role and the composition was either broken up into shorter thematic fragments linked with the words, or it was totally subordinated to the declamation, so that a new type of pseudopolyphony and homophony was born. Leonhard Lechner (c. 1553–1606), Jakob Reiner (1560–1606), Hans Leo Hassler (1564–1612), Jakob Handl (also known as Gallus, 1550–1591), and others produced a new art by combining the currents flowing in from Italy. They gave fuller expression to the text by means of an art that employed both the strict polyphony of the Netherland school and the word treatment of the madrigalists. This personal interpretation of the text with its musical embroidery was art alien to the liturgical attitude. Hence the outcry for a more liturgical conception and a plainer representation of the words. From the turn of the sixteenth century there was widespread interest in the problem of church music.

POLYPHONY AS LITURGICAL EXPRESSION

Church music was again regarded primarily as an ecclesiastico-liturgical art. The ecclesiastical pronouncements regarding church music at synods and provincial councils became more numerous. They stressed again and again the liturgical link, and characterized as improper the independent musical evolution with its personal interpretation and the purely musical embroidery of the text. They brought up the question of a reform of the entire church-music field, involving the reorientation of all those who had anything to do with church music. The remodeling of the liturgical melodies of the *cantus Gregorianus* and the re-evaluation of all the texts resulted. Tropes, sequences and *cantiones* were sacrificed, and complicated polyphony where the text no longer appeared in the liturgical sense was outlawed.

Another danger for polyphonic church music came from the Protestant

Reformation. Many groups promoted church songs in the vernacular, as an expression of popular piety, in contrast to Catholic music with its liturgical ties. On the other hand other reformers banned all free practice of art, as in Puritanism or in Calvinism which only retained the Huguenot Psalter. The organ was forbidden by Zwinglians and Calvinists. In these tumultuous times ideas such as these also influenced Catholic thinking and further complicated the already tangled position of church music. Just as in the fourteenth century the novelties in the musical sphere led to a general reassertion of the Church's position in the decree of Pope John XXII, so the many-faceted position of church music in the sixteenth century demanded some sort of definition or settlement by the Church.

The Council of Trent, in treating liturgical problems, made a decision with regard to music after Cardinals Charles Borromeo, Vitellius Vitellozzo and Otto Truchsess von Waldburg had prepared the question beforehand in Rome. Only a few of the decrees concerning church music were actually formulated and individual technical problems were not treated at all; but the important point, besides the establishment of the liturgical texts, was that polyphony, which had been attacked by many, was formally recognized along with the medieval liturgical melodies, but on condition that profane traits (*lascivum et impurum*) be avoided and the texts be understandable. An example of compositions that offered the text a suitable garb by a coupling of homophony and polyphony was the conciliar *Preces* of Jacobus de Kerle (1532–1591), composed at the instigation of Cardinal Truchsess von Waldburg. They were sung at the procession of the cardinals and were favorably received and probably helped the fathers of the Council to take a favorable stand on contemporary ecclesiastical polyphony.

J. de Kerle, Responsorium II pro Concilio

PALESTRINA

In Palestrina's work the conflict between text and music, between the horizontal and vertical tensions in the composition, between counterpoint and harmony, reached its most important solution. By his work Giovanni Pierluigi da Palestrina (1525–1594) created a new church-music ideal.

Beginning about the middle of the sixteenth century composers employed polyphonic and homophonic devices side by side, proceeding in part from an emphasis on music, in part from an interpretation of the text. Thus alternately they took an objective or subjective stand with regard to the text. But now the consideration of a liturgical ideal brought about a stylistic compromise. Both horizontal and vertical tensions were equally stressed; the words were marked according to their grammatical accentuation and not overlaid with melismas. Thus the humanistic striving for declamation was given a place within the bounds of polyphony but in all the various voices. However the textual expression did not lead to a personal interpretation but rather to a general stylizing of the words in the music. This effort for an objective expression of the liturgical text created a stylistic compromise which was not sought in profane music, at least not in the same degree. Consequently profane music in the sixteenth century, exemplified in the madrigal, chanson and German lied, reached its highest development in a subjective evaluation of the text. This was easily achieved by the homophonic style of expression and the employing of chamber music and solo voice forms.

Palestrina's motets and masses, among them the famous *Missa Papae Marcelli*, achieved a perfect illumination of the text with a homophonic-polyphonic homogeneity of composition. Starting from a contrapuntal style of interlacing voices, the technique used in his earliest works, Palestrina created a new ideal of ecclesiastical writing. He resolved the conflict between the horizontal line and the vertical structure by means of the triad, and at the same time he succeeded in reconciling the style of text declamation with the devices of polyphonic writing. The ideal thus achieved kept Palestrina's name alive for centuries, even in times that had little or no appreciation or understanding of the stylistic solution he evolved. In the preface to his masses, 1567, he himself made mention of a *novum genus musicum*. It meant assembling all the stylistic tendencies of his age and recasting them into the unity of an ideal style which could produce the text-music compromise sought by the Council of Trent. To shape this homogeneous polyphonic style, adjustments in many previous devices and techniques were necessary. The composer had to divide the composition according to the phrases of the text; he had to create the melodic phrases according to the words; he had to select a rhythm proportioned to the verbal accent; and he had to maintain the independence of each voice line within the declamation structure. These techniques demonstrate the dominant position of the text in this style of Palestrina, in contrast to the violence frequently done the words by the early Netherlanders in their contrapuntal settings or by the isorhythmic devices of an earlier period.

2nd Book of Motets

Just as the text influenced the musical composition, so also the various principles of writing left their imprint on the setting. For example, contrapuntal voice leading, the movement of the melody within certain tonal groups, and the underlying harmonic background were considered. In addition, leading factors in composition were the creating of motifs within the limitation demanded, the stressing of tonal centers, and the utilization of isorhythmic combinations in all voices. Thus a style was produced for motets and masses that was both the high point of the polyphonic style and the foundation for the growth of new musical principles that could pave the way for entirely new paths. Its expressive values were later evolved in various directions.

THE "PALESTRINA STYLE"

If Palestrina was able to create an ideal compromise between text and music by reviving the liturgical spirit, it was the achievement of the Spanish priest, Tomás Luis da Victoria (1540–1613), to discover the most effective means of expressing the text musically. He used an almost unrestrained vocabulary of harmonies, employing new media in his melodic and tonal structure.

Spaniards had already contributed valuable additions to the treasury of polyphonic church music in the creations of Cristobal Morales (1500–1553), Bartolomeo Escobedo (c. 1510–1563), and Francisco Guerrero (1528–1599).

The idealization of textual expression and its musical conformation was further developed by Giovanni Maria Nanino (1545–1607), Felice

Victoria

Anerio (1560–1614), Francesco Suriano (1549–1620), Matteo Asola (✝1609), Giovanni Croce (1557–1609), Marc Antonio Ingegnieri (1545–1592), Costanzo Porta (1530–1601), and others. These efforts toward an objective textual expression in musical form were already to be found in Palestrina's predecessors, Costanzo Festa (✝1545) and Giovanni Animuccia (c. 1500–1571). Among the Netherlanders, Philippe de Monte (1521–1603) especially endeavored to attain the ideal textual treatment of church music by rich-sounding, compact settings. The liturgical consideration, combined with a humanistic concept of textual development, prodded composers everywhere to try with every available means for a more profound expression of the text. Giovanni Gabrieli (1557–1612) promoted this expression in musical forms by an extension of tonal media. Orlando di Lasso (also known as Roland de Lassus, c. 1532–1594), however, used the new stylistic media in a more personal interpretative expression with more dramatic effect. The refinement of textual representation turned from grammatical correctness and clarity of text to characterization of its contents as a whole. Then began a new practice in an attempt to make the greatest use of the expressive ideas inherent in the text itself. Composers desired to transfer these to the music, not just for an individual word here and there, but in an over-all effective interpretation of the entire text. This tone-painting technique was in contrast to the more objective method employed previously in setting texts. It soon became the fashion to utilize this expressive representation. Numerous lesser composers who associated themselves with the new polyphony used this fashion for all it was worth, so that in the end polyphonic church music was practically paralyzed. This was all the more significant because polyphony had provided a second essential form for church music alongside Gregorian chant and it should have had universal validity. But like the further developments in Gregorian chant, vocal polyphony had put its stamp on an essential direction in church music. Later on it came to terms with more contemporary church-music styles. The vocal polyphony of the sixteenth century — the Palestrinan style — was thus a point of departure for two basic tendencies in multivoiced church music. On the one hand contemporary church music constructed on the foundation of polyphony the *stile moderno*, which took up the precise themes of polyphony and homophony, and joined them to declamation. This is exemplified in the church music of Matteo Asola (✠1609), Vincenzo Ruffo (1554–1587), Luca Marenzio (1550–1599), and many others. By multiplying expressive forms in polychoral writing and the use of instruments, this *stile moderno* followed the lead of the Venetians and Romans. It took such steps in harmonic expansion that at last, in the monody of Ludovico Grossi da Viadana (1564–1645), Antonio Cifra (1584–1629) and others, the break with older forms was complete. On the other hand the Palestrina style led to a further cultivation of the vocal polyphony in its original form, called the *stile antico*. It utilized means of transformations and imitations that were only to some degree determined by contemporary movements.

The Counter Reformation movement within the Church had drawn church music back to its proper sphere in worship and enlisted its artistic values in the movement for reform. This produced the foundation for the idealization of church music as expressed by Palestrina and his circle. At the same time the basis was laid for an emphasis on extraliturgical religious music in the motet, the sacred madrigal and the oratorio. St. Philip Neri, by means of his oratorio, created a solemn form that was religious without being liturgical, a form whose influence was quite important during the breakdown of thought and life in the middle of the sixteenth century. Animuccia and Palestrina were his musical collaborators. This oratorio movement, to which numerous religious works of Roman composers owe their origin, soon picked up traits of the new art. Anerio's *Teatro armonico* likewise lay in this direction, as did Emilio del Cavalieri's (c. 1550–1602) *Rappresentazione di anima e di corpo* (1600), the Jesuit plays, the spiritual *cantate*, and the sacred oratorio which now grew into a specialized musical form. But the choir of the Sistine Chapel remained a nursery for a strict *a cappella* style of church music. Right down to our own time this tradition has been preserved there and the absence of organ and instruments has continued uninterrupted.

CHURCH MUSIC IN THE NEW WORLD

With the very first Spanish colonial foundations the Americas were brought into contact with plain chant and polyphony. For many centuries, even to the present day, church music in Latin America was subject to both the virtues and the defects of the Spanish and Portuguese development. Musically, the sixteenth century was an era of solid foundation and great progress in the colonies. The first solemn Mass sung in America was celebrated at San Domingo in 1494. In Mexico City, by 1519, a church-music school had already been set up by the Netherlander, Francesco Petrus van Gent, and through this foundation the music of the great Spanish classical polyphonists, Victoria, Guerrero and Morales was spread, together with the works of Lassus and Palestrina.

Juan Pablas set up the first American printing press in Mexico City, in 1539. The initial musical project, an *Ordinarium*, appeared in 1556, and nine similar volumes were published by 1604. Most of the music was plain chant, although Juan Navarro,[1] the cathedral choirmaster, at-

[1] Juan Navarro was born in Cadiz and should not be confused with a Juan Navarro of Seville who never left Spain.

tempted several pieces of polyphony, including settings of the Passion. The style of these few compositions is indistinguishable from that of the then current conservative style of Spanish church music.

The earliest composer of church polyphony in the Western hemisphere about whom we have definite information was Fernando Franco (✠1585), who was born in Alcantara, a few miles from the Portuguese border. He came to the New World about 1554, and was active in Guatemala and as *maestro di cappella* of the cathedral in Mexico City from 1575 until his death ten years later. His extant works include several settings of the *Magnificat* and the *Salve Regina*, as well as miscellaneous hymns and responsories. Some of his music, used by the missionaries in teaching the Indians, has a text in the Nahuatl language. Of significance, too, is the fact that as early as 1583, an Aztec translation of the *Psalmodia Christiana* of Bernardino de Sahagun was produced.

Toward the end of the sixteenth century and in the opening years of the seventeenth, the growing body of European instrumental music began to be heard in America, thanks to the efforts of the unending stream of missionaries. Organs were built, especially in capital cities, and the music of Antonio de Cabezán was performed in Lima and in Mexico City by 1586, only eight years after its appearance in Spain. Wherever cathedral centers were built, music schools in the European tradition were attached, with systematic training in chant and polyphony.

The more popular elements of Spanish music were inevitably brought in too. Hymns, called *alabados*, in the style of the Spanish *romanza*, became popular, especially through the efforts of A. Margil de Jesús (1657–1726). The religious drama, especially what is known as the *auto sacramental* (and which was stylistically akin to the Italian oratorio), had a vigorous impact on the population.

III Music at Worship

CHAPTER 11

Baroque Art

EAGERNESS FOR A NEW POLYPHONIC STYLE

The various creative forms of the sixteenth century revealed a new vital feeling which led to the more personalized baroque characterization of the liturgical text. The symmetry of the Renaissance concept of text and tone gave place in the baroque era to an increasing appreciation of verbal expressiveness. This baroque attitude made use of every existing means of expression and even endeavored to create new ones. Already as early as the middle of the sixteenth century this tendency was becoming more and more pronounced; it made itself manifest in the abandoning of strict polyphonic work with its free-rhythmic declamatory forms as well as in the increase of the inner tension of the composition by harmonic innovations. It was the expressive effort that framed the composition and thus overrode the manneristic principles of the stylistic compromise of the classic polyphonic period. *Musica poetica* and *musica reservata* became the catchwords for this new movement that stood side by side with the stylistic compromise of Jacobus de Kerle, Philippe de Monte, and of Palestrina and his circle. This new movement, however, still felt itself more or less bound to the expressive forms of the old polyphonic composition.

Orlando di Lasso (c. 1532–1594) stands at the very center of this new art of the sixteenth century. The very fact that his motets (over 1200) outnumber his masses is an indication that his main interest was the musical representation of the occasional and different. His ideal was not the interpretation of the uniform, unchanging texts of the ordinary of the Mass, even though his more than fifty masses are works of the most profound expressiveness. It was rather the constantly changing tonal possibilities and the novel contents of the many motets that roused him to utilize all the cosmopolitan gifts of expression with which he was endowed. Thus he took many a bold stroke, breaking down old forms and stirring up a desire to discover further tensions in the music, by a fuller use of chromatics, the widening of intervals, and by forms of declamation that differed from the ideal but offered new possibilities. He utilized parlando-type phrases and interchange of homophony and polyphony. If at times the experimental mood overrode the necessity for an increase in the personalized expression and thus led to remarkable compositional forms, the result of such attempts was, in the end, made to serve in shaping a new art of expression.

Christe Dei, Motet by Lasso

This personalized art naturally freed itself as much as possible from the Gregorian *cantus firmus.* The thematic material was used to create a closed form, the final development of the Netherlanders' technique of composition.

Although Orlando di Lasso shaped his art within the limits of polyphony, his church music was not free from elaborations of expressiveness through harmonic tensions, parlando effects and free rhythm, the interchange of homophony and polyphony and the overlapping of both these forms. There was a definite influence of secular art on his church music. Although these devices are more frequent in his chansons and madrigals, he does not hesitate to express the liturgical texts by the same forceful means and thereby broaden the stylistic media. Thus Orlando di Lasso created the unusual in his church music, without deteriorating into mere mannerism. With Luca Marenzio (1550–1599), Jakob Handl (also known as Jacobus Gallus, 1550–1591), and others, the motet was further developed, but it was a motet which forsook the clear lucidity of the polyphonic expression of Palestrina. In this art the determining factor was the text.

For the sake of the text and textual expressiveness, the symmetry of the setting was destroyed, and the homophonic parlando device was introduced even in strict composition. The text assumed the leading role and grew more and more dominating. As a result the voices were no longer arranged in the order of free polyphony but in conjunction with the main voice, which was tied to the text. The independence of the declamatory-rhythmical accents of the individual voices was sacrificed in favor of simultaneous accentuation and declamation in all voices. The composition, deprived of the possibility of movement in counterpoint and declamatory rhythm, was vitalized by harmonic tensions through the introduction of altered tones, and by elaboration through the polychoral technique. The effects achieved by the grouping of various voice combinations grew out of the polyphonic style, but soon expanded. In the plastic arts, new spatial effects were being discovered, and this was transferred to music. Voices were grouped and spaced, and in turn, choirs were separated to produce the effect of space. These *cori spezzati* alternated with each other in much the same way that the individual voices had interplayed in the polyphonic style.

INCREASE OF EXPRESSIVENESS

Although Adrien Willaert (c. 1490–1562) must be credited with the creation of the polychoral art — the use of several separate choirs — it was Giovanni Gabrieli (1557–1612) who determined the purely tonal forces of this form of composition.

Gio. Gabrieli, Cantica sacra no. 4 1597

This form of expression was further developed in Venice and Rome. Paolo Agostini (1593–1627) and Antonio Maria Abbatini (1595–1677) created polychoral church-music compositions for as many as twelve choirs; Virgilio Mazzocchi (✝1648) massed his choirs right up to the dome of St. Peter's. It was Orazio Benevoli (1605–1672), however, who reached the very peak of tonal massiveness with his fifty-three-voiced festive mass for the consecration of the cathedral of Salzburg in 1628. In such a multiplication of voices the free movement of parts was impossible. The simplest method of composition was to double the octaves; this was recommended for the bass by Giovanni Maria Artusi (1581), and for all the voices by Praetorius (1614), Viadana (1612), and Giovanni Maria Capello (1613).

To this increase in vocal sound was added an increase in instrumental sound, as the two media were linked. The instruments provided a *colla parte* accompaniment, but in addition there was the organ that supplied an instrumental tonal re-enforcement of the whole. At the same time the organ brought about the reduction of the voice harmonies to chords and chordal progressions. Since this type of accompaniment was used not only with homophonic choruses but also for polyphonic works, even in Palestrina's lifetime, the original horizontal tension of the voices was given a new interpretation in terms of a harmonic-chordal base. Since this chordal reduction of the *bassus ad organum* represented the fullness of tonal resources as much as the polyphonic piece itself, there was a possibility of giving a complete performance of a polyphonic composition even when only a few of the voices were sung and the others were left out. When some of the parts were missing, a substitution was made not by playing the missing voices *instrumentaliter* and thus inserting them into the full composition, but merely by presenting the harmonic base of the composition without paying any attention to the contrapuntal leading of the voices.

MONODY

Although this practice had already become a common method for presenting church music even in the last decades of the sixteenth century, it was left to Ludovico Grossi da Viadana (1564–1645), in his *Cento concerti ecclesiastici* (1602) to offer a new form of composition consciously built on this principle.

The chordal accompaniment was thus written as a thorough-bass or *basso continuo*, giving external expression to the vertical structure of the harmonies. This new kind of composition made it possible not only to present the text clearly but to give it enlarged expression in a sololike design. Although the formation of the melody originally followed the principles of polyphonic melody, the solo-style mobility of the voice soon brought about the abandonment of this basis.

From the viewpoint of declamation, new impulses in this direction came from ideas that had developed in the sphere of the Florentine *Camerata*. Following the humanistic notion of verbal declamation, these ideas crystallized in a new melodic development that took the extreme form of a rhythmically stylized recitative. This meant forsaking the basic laws of melody to find a new kind of textual shaping in the parlando recitative, which in turn, already in the work of Giulio Caccini, sought a link with the ancient forms of melody. Church music possessed a similar stylizing of text in the psalmodic recitative. This free declamation, determined only by the text, was given a harmonic setting in fauxbourdon.

1st Tone · · · · · · · · · · · · · · · · · · Cäsar de Zachariis (1590)

Monodic church music was not sympathetic to the extreme declamatory forms of the Florentine monodists, who paid absolutely no attention to melodic development. Church music also slackened the monodic manner of expression created by Viadana by linking it with parlando-style declamation until the separation of arioso and recitative sections made possible an independent development of both forms. Beginning about 1605, numerous works appeared that went beyond Viadana in melodic-declamatory mobility and developed the new style. Ottavio Durante, in his *Arie devote* (1608) and Johannes Kapsberger in his *Motetti passegiatti* (1612), indicated by their very titles the personal nature of their art.

A. Agazzari, Et repleti sunt 1614

The principle of declamation and its musical delineation gave rise to a new type of construction and form which moved beyond the solo motet to the multimembered *cantata*. This *concertante* art of the *cantata*, first practiced in Italy, soon gained access into the church music of all countries. Ivan Lukačič (1574–1648), Kapellmeister in Split, and by origin a Dalmatian Croat, adopted this emotion packed style of declamation in his *Sacrae cantiones* (1620), as did the Polish church composers of this period, for example, Nicholas Zielenski (*Offertoria et communiones,* 1611), Martin Mielczewski (✝1651), and others.

Lukačič, Cantato Domino

Ju - cun - dum sit e - i e - lo - qui - um me-

um e - go ve - ro de - lec - ta - bor in Do - mi-

no e - go ve - ro de - lec - ta - - - - - -

- bor de - lec-ta - - - - - - bor in Do-mi - no

These new stylistic media were found useful for functional church music not only because they answered the quest for new modes of expression but because they simplified the work of performance. The *obbligato* organ part became the main support and the small number of voices accommodated the declining resources of the choir. Thus all that was needed for church-music purposes was an organist and a few soloists. It was possible to omit the heavy work of preparing a choir, especially after women's voices were gradually admitted to the performance of church music in the seventeenth century. Thus there was a nexus between the introduction of the new art and the decline of choir schools, which were retained only in the larger churches, and even here they lost their importance in favor of soloists. When the choir work lost its footing in church music, instruments won greater importance. Their original subsidiary position was transformed into a necessary accompaniment (*obbligato*). As early as 1611, Bartolommeo Castoreo relates that in the churches of Rome instruments had already for some time been taken for granted. Church music changed its whole character and what was originally a monodic art aimed at enhancing the text in solo fashion now gradually was overwhelmed by instrumental forms. As a result of this development the voice parts assumed an instrumental style both in melody and form and adopted instrumental themes.

Thus, around 1600, a fundamental break occurred in church music both in setting and expression. Emotionalism had created not only new forms but new possibilities of expression which, because of their subjective tendency, drew church music away more and more from its liturgical ties. Divine worship came to be regarded as the external scene for the development of musical media.

CONCERTANTE CHURCH MUSIC

In Italy the great synthesis of the different elements in church music growing out of the baroque attitude was the work of Claudio Monteverdi and, later, of Giacomo Carissimi. From a multitude of elements they created a new basis for church-music expression which had a determining effect on its further development. Of significance in evaluating the fundamental change in the attitude toward church music in the middle of the seventeenth century is the fact that in the inventories and catalogs of this period, with few exceptions, polyphonic church compositions of the sixteenth century have disappeared.

Although in the new art polyphony was no longer regarded as the strictly ideal form, there was a proportionately stronger tie to Gregorian chant as an external indication of the ecclesiastical character of the music. Monteverdi (1567–1643) frequently used the chant as *cantus firmus* or as thematic material, or he freely interposed it in the setting. Thus his new style obtained a definite link with liturgical song and at the same time secured its justification as music for worship.

As in opera, so also in church music, Monteverdi created a new principle of musical expression. The *stile concitato* had become entwined with the old *cantus firmus* work. It was no longer restricted to the simple solo accompanied by the thorough-bass but even invaded the multivoiced composition. What was essential to this art was not the new melodic style nor the declamation but the new effort at expressiveness, the search for a dramatic interpretation of the text, and consequently the quest for new media of expression. In order to describe holy awe in his *Duo seraphim,*

C. Monteverdi, Magnificat

Monteverdi chose the theme that follows, employing it in the various voices. It is easy to see how far the means of musical delineation had moved from the old principle of composition and this in a work that appeared in 1610, just sixteen years after Palestrina's death.

In Monteverdi's *Psalms* there was a combination of the *concertante* choir style of Gabrieli with solo parlando, creating a new synthesis of setting and expression. Concertized masses and motets came to the fore. Adriano Banchieri (1574–1634), Alessandro de Grandi (✝1630), Tarquinio Merula (✝1650), Francesco Turini (1590–1656), Giovanni Rovetta (✝1688), Marco da Zanobi Gagliano (c. 1575–1642) in their ecclesiastical works formed new modes of expression that aimed at contrasting treatments of sound. Out of the multitude of such devices, from solo to multivoiced choir, from simple thorough-bass accompaniment to full orchestral setting, the *duette* and *soli* with concerted instruments became the most prominent. This art was characterized not by simple representation of the text but by a dramatic interpretation in declamation and musical setting. The designation *affetti* for such works stressed their basic attitude which, because it was symptomatic of the times, soon took the lead in all countries. Baroque splendor and the emotionalized declamation and tonal effects soon changed the simple songs of the early monodists into grand forms. Gregor Aichinger (1564–1628), Bernhard Klingenstein (1545–1614), Johannes Khuen (1605–1680), Johann Stadlmayr (1560–1648), Christoph Strauss, Abraham Megerle (1607–1680), A. Holtzner, and others were the proponents of this change of style in Germany, although the Thirty Years' War probably put many obstacles in the way of its further development. Heinrich Schütz was the great promoter of this art in non-Catholic northern Germany.

The overlapping of *concertante* tonal effects and solo-style art soon led to pronounced contrasts in forms, although these served to enliven the setting. Contrast used as a means of increasing the expression, a feature already provided in the sixteenth century, was further broadened by the introduction of solo compositions. Thus in one work forms that contrasted in style and expression were placed side by side, and they in turn developed in their own fashion, growing more and more apart.

The solo style was divided into declamatory recitative and arioso melody. The choral style set declamatory sections with chords next to polyphonic settings that elaborated themes in the old fashion or declamatory themes of the *stile affettuoso*, with or without orchestral accompaniment. The cantata, both in ecclesiastical and in secular art, managed to blend this variety of artistic shapes into a formal unity, giving to each type a particular expression. In this way church music took on a new shape that dominated the second half of the seventeenth century.

Giacomo Carissimi (1604–1674), who by extending the scope of the cantata made the religious oratorio the most important form in the new manner, promoted this expressive form in his church music. Through his numerous pupils, Alessandro Scarlatti (in Italy), Johann Kaspar Kerll (in Germany) and Marc Antoine Charpentier (in France), all of whom became leading figures, he was instrumental in bringing about further developments in church music.

The generation of church musicians born at the start of the seventeenth century was at one with Carissimi in establishing the new expressive value of the *solo tutti* technique in the cantata form. The stylistic media were already provided. It was now the goal of the various movements to utilize

G. Carissimi

them in the service of expressive form. There were three such movements: the *stile antico* busied itself with continuing the *a cappella* art; the *stile moderno* kept searching out new forms; and the *stile misto* sought to combine both of these styles.

CHAPTER 12

Stile Moderno, Stile Antico

SPLIT IN CHURCH MUSIC STYLES

The sentimentality and the ideal of piety that came to the front during the baroque era shaped new forms of expression at the start of the seventeenth century. The multivoiced ecclesiastical style — the ideal style of ancient classical polyphony — continued to be cultivated in the traditional fashion, along with the new stylistic forms. This did not mean so much the performance of the original works of the sixteenth century as new attempts in this style, known as the *stile antico,* in which the old forms were to be given new life along the lines of the new efforts at expressiveness. Because of the sharp contrast in attitude between the two styles, the original form was soon overwhelmed; this was to be expected, considering the peculiar situation of church music at that time. Thus a stylistic division occurred during the seventeenth century, which was to continue in church music till the romantic period. This was particularly noticeable in Italian music. The *bel canto* development of the *stile moderno* promoted a separation from ecclesiastical expression and thus involved a strict divorce from the conservative *a cappella* style.

THE NEW ECCLESIASTICAL STYLE

In form and expression the cantata was predominant in the *stile moderno.* The Italians developed in particular the solo setting, flexibility of the

119

melody, and the declamatory parlando. Special opportunities were offered this development by the preference for just a few voices, as in the work of Bonifazio Graziani (1605–1664), Francesco Cavalli (1602–1676), Maurizio Cazzati (1620–1677), Antonio Draghi (1635–1700), Agostino Steffani (1654–1728), and many others who gave ever freer rein to the development. Expressive coloratura was expanded, especially among the Bologna masters, until at the beginning of the eighteenth century it was utilized in a new sense by the Neopolitans. The choral setting was generally subordinated to the declamatory lead of the upper voice; in other words the choral part preferred a declamatory solution of the harmonic setting.

In Germany it was the *concertante* choir style that was developed. Declamatory themes, elaborated in the manner of the old polyphonic setting, gave shape to a new choir setting. Carissimi's pupil, Johann Kasper Kerll (1627–1693), was the leader in this art which never won much support in Italy. Heinrich Schmeltzer (c. 1623–1680), Franz Heinrich Biber (1644–1704), Christoph Strauss, and others also cultivated this choral form. Following the model of the cantata, it was often interspersed with solo parts. By using these contrasting media, a synthetic form was developed.

This contrapuntal handling of the voices produced a compact compression, with movement provided in the instrument. Running basses as well as *ostinati* thus won importance, as did free melody, broken chords, fanfare motifs, etc. The *solo tutti* division was the predominant technique

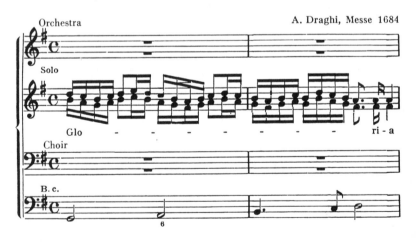

Stile Moderno, Stile Antico

in choir and orchestra; the development remained restricted to the *concertino* while the *ripieni* were added as an enlargement of the tonal resources in occasional sections. At other times polyphonic sections in the *stile antico* took their place. Even the Italians working in German courts, like Giovanni Valentini (organist in Vienna, 1619), Antonio Bertali (1605–1699), Felice Sances (1600–1679), Stefano Bernardi (c. 1575–1638), and others developed this form of setting.

J. K. Kerll, Dignare me (1669)

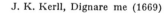

The focal point was no longer to be found in the setting as such, but in the emotional interpretation of its language. For this reason the art was employed in strict liturgical music but also in more personal religious music where greater individual expression was possible. Thus it unfolded into the church cantata, the *sepolcri* (i.e., Passion music), etc. This provided the bridge from church music to the oratorio which in turn gradually assumed the forms of the opera.

Originally a simple harmonic support, the thorough-bass was now embodied in the setting thematically. The concertizing instruments gained independence of movement and liberation from the vocal theme. This opened the way to the instrumentalization of the whole composition, while at the same time there was a restriction of the choir in favor of solo work.

France adopted neither the free melodic formation of Italy nor the contrapuntal choral work of Germany but instead shaped a dramatic church music on the basis of its own principles of declamation. Declamatory stylization and a compromise between aria and recitative, by means of this declamation, created a rigid and, at times, pathetic setting in which both the play of tonal colors and any compelling flow of melody were missing.

Solo-Motet, Splendor aeternae gloriae, by Pierre Robert (1618-1699)

This tendency to stylize the setting characterized also multivoiced compositions. However, in their own peculiar style the motets of Jean Baptiste Lully (1632–1687), Henri Dumont (1610–1684) and their contemporaries display a profoundly ecclesiastical seriousness.

From No. 27 of the Cantica Sacra (1652) by H. Dumont

In the works of Guillaume Bouzignac, Nicolas Formé, and others, the ecclesiastical style in France at the beginning of the seventeenth century moved toward freer forms along the lines of the Italian concerto, but their efforts were soon suppressed. It was not till the beginning of the eighteenth century that the mixture of Italian and French forms of expression gained momentum in French church music. French church music preserved its vocal orientation. In Italian music, on the contrary, the instrumental style was not confined to the ritornels and other independent instrumental sections but determined the whole composition.

INSTRUMENTAL MUSIC FOR CHURCH

For the position of instrumental music in church this was of fundamental importance. With this change of emphasis it was but a short step to introduce into the service independent instrumental compositions along with, or instead of, vocal compositions. The church sonata, as well as the development of independent organ music, became the means by which instrumental music gained a footing in church. About the turn of the eighteenth century, a type of music was created in Italy known as the church sonata. In several movements it contained a *grave*, in duple time, with both homophonic and imitative sections; an *allegro*, in duple time, that was fugal; a homophonic, slow movement in triple meter; and a fast closing movement, fugal and generally in duple meter. Giovanni Battista Vitali, Arcangelo Corelli, Antonio Caldara, and Evaristo Felice dall'Abaco were active in transforming and refining the trio sonata into the *sonata da chiesa*, which soon discarded its church connection and became a general form for instruments. In Poland the church sonata was adopted by the Cistercian Stanislaus Szarzyński. His countryman, Martin Mielczewski, writing in the first half of the seventeenth century, had already composed instrumental *canzoni* for church purposes.

The decline in the sense of what was fitting for liturgical worship made possible the practice in the seventeenth century of using instrumental compositions in place of settings of the Proper. The breakdown in forms made possible the switch from instrumental church compositions to free instrumental pieces in church, especially instrumental soli. Finally there came the adoption into the church of all secular instrumental art (overture, symphony, sonata, and suite). With the coming program music, as in the pastoral compositions or the introductory fanfares and marches, the adoption of such instrumental works into the service became all the easier.

ORGAN PLAYING

Church organ music, too, grew independent of the liturgical melodies and free from a connection with vocal music. General forms of instrumental music presented organ music with new possibilities of development. From the sixteenth century on, the organ had gradually gained importance in the performance of liturgical song. It had not only altered the Gregorian chant through the accompaniment, but to some extent it had replaced it by the practice known as alternation. The simple recitation of the liturgical text to the accompaniment of a short organ piece called the verset — a form that continued to develop — offered the opportunity for giving it a purely musical shape and weaning it away from the Gregorian melodies which, in this period, were gradually lost or at least transformed. In southern Germany, Jacob Froberger (1615–1667), Alessandro Poglietti (✠1683), Johann Kaspar Kerll (1627–1693), and Georg and Gottlieb Muffat (1645–1704; 1690–1770) were the leading masters of ecclesiastical organ music.

The most important function of the Catholic organist was improvising. Designed to fill in the pauses in the service as well as to introduce the singing, improvisation eventually led to uninterrupted musical activity throughout the whole service. The organ accompanied the priest's chants, the Gregorian chants, and even played during the elevation. To fulfill this task the church organ registration was continually expanded and tonal forces were added. In Italy and south Germany composition for the church organ was broadened from the *ricercare* and *canzone* to free forms, which soon lost every association with ecclesiastical expression. In Spain and France the liturgical melody at first continued to hold its leading role. The tradition of Jean Titelouze (1563–1633) was continued by Guillaume Nivers (1617–1703), Nicholas Gigault (c. 1645-1700), Nicolas Lebègue (1630–1702), André Raison, François Couperin and others, until in the works of Claude Daquin (1694–1772) and Jacques Marie Beauvarlet-Charpentier (1766–1834), among others, it gradually turned into a free composition estranged from the ecclesiastical style.

While the organ music intended for Catholic service gradually changed in the eighteenth century and grew shallower, in central and north Germany the organ art of the Lutheran service continued to develop. Fugue and choral prelude found in Johann Sebastian Bach (1685–1750) an unexcelled exponent.

Organ construction developed an ideal of tone corresponding to this evolution affecting the organ's place in the service. In north Germany organ builders, under the influence of Arp Schnitger (1648–1720), E. Casparini (✠1706), and others, stressed clarity of tone in their work. South German builders under Josef Gabler (1700–1784), M. Riepp, Franz Xavier Krismann (✠1795), and others sought for orchestral tone coloring. With Andreas and Gottfried Silbermann (1678–1734; 1683–1753), German organ building reached its height. In France organ building was principally concerned with the coloristic and invitative voices of the organ. Dom Bédos de Celles (1706–1779) wrote a large manual on the art of organ building.

NEO-GREGORIAN COMPOSITIONS

Like the *stile moderno* in vocal church music, organ music for the Catholic service continued to develop ever freer musical forms that gradually drew apart from the specific purposes of worship. Opposed to this tendency to secularize church music was a counter-movement that tried to cultivate a definite ecclesiastical outlook. It endeavored to preserve Gregorian chant, emphasizing its similarity to the contemporary principles of declamation and melody. At the same time it destroyed the essential feature of this medieval art and invented remarkable new compositions that could be called chant only because they used the old notation. These were placed side by side with ancient melodies which were themselves altered almost beyond recognition.

Mass of Bordeaux

Ky - - - ri - e   e - - - - - - - -

e - - - - - - - - - - le - i - son

This movement to alter the medieval melodies and to create new ones in line with contemporary fashions was cultivated especially in the circle of the Oratorians. This modernization of the ancient Gregorian is found in the writings on Gregorian theory of Pierre Benoit de Jumilhac (1673), Jean Jacques Souhaithy (1677), Paul d'Amance (1701) and many others. Compositions in this style by Henri Dumont (1685) were the most popular.

Missa regia by Dumont

A-gnus De - i qui tol - lis pec-ca - ta mun - di mi - se - re - re no - bis

The ecclesiastical modal system disintegrated through the introduction of accidentals, and the current tonic-dominant tension of the major-minor system replaced it.

ECCLESIASTICAL A CAPPELLA ART

The conservative tendency that sought to cultivate the chant also fostered the *a cappella* style that had come to be thought of as ideal church art. The old *a cappella* works of the sixteenth century were provided with a thorough-bass. In the new compositions that utilized the expressional media of the sixteenth-century polyphonic art, accompaniment by orchestra or organ was taken for granted. Of significance in evaluating the new church music of the seventeenth century is the fact that nearly all composers wrote for church not only in the *stile moderno* but also in the *stile antico*. Michael Praetorius (1619) and Giovanni Ghizzolo (1625) expressly designated this old style as *a cappella* in contrast to the concerto of the modern style. Canon and *cantus firmus* gave this form of composition archaic interest and at times, too, the impression of scholarliness. This *stile antico*, which was indeed thoroughly different from the ancient classical polyphony in its expression, its formation of theme and melody, and especially in the way it used declamation and harmony, was not merely a secondary, antiquarian phenomenon in church music. On the contrary, it rightly stood on a par with the *stile moderno*. It was not a stiff museum conception but rather an artistic development. This style of writing is found in works conceived throughout as *stile antico*, but it was also used to develop contrast in works employing the *stile moderno*. In the *stile misto* a compromise was sought between the basic forms of the old and the new styles. This distinction made by theoreticians at the beginning of the eighteenth century merely recognized practices already in use in the seventeenth century.

The direct tradition of Palestrina was still at work in the compositions of Felice and Francesco Anerio (1550–1614; 1567–1620), of Francesco Suriano (1549–1620), and of Giovanni Maria and Giovanni Bernardino Nanini (1545–1607; 1559–1623). It continued to be an influence in the creations of Gregorio Allegri (1584–1652), Orazio Benevoli (1602–1672), Antonio Cifra (1575–1638), Antonio Abbatini (1595–1677), Francesco Foggia (1605–1688), Romano Micheli (1575–1655), Pier Francesco Valentini (✝1654), Matteo Simonelli, and others. Harmony and tonality in these works, however, took account of the new tendencies. The northern Italian composers adapted the strict *stile antico* by using declamation and harmony. Maurizio Cazzati (1620–1677), Francesco della Porta (1590–1666), Pietro Andrea and Marc Antonio Ziani (c. 1630–1711; 1653–1715), and others, like the Roman composers, continued the division between the old and new styles, but endeavored to combine traits of the *stile moderno* with the *a cappella* style.

In Germany, where the work of Orlando di Lasso and his contemporaries was preserved in numerous collections till the middle of the seventeenth century, the *stile antico* was widely used. The strict but very expressive composition of Johann Stadlmayr (1560–1648), Abraham Megerle (1607–1680) and others is a paragon of the southern German *a cappella* art of the seventeenth century. It adopted in declamation and melody many of the traits of the new art.

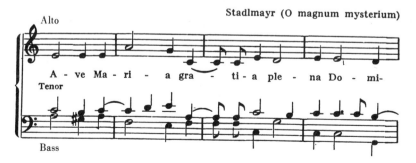

Stadlmayr (O magnum mysterium)

Canon and *cantus firmus* forms were readily combined with the *a cappella* structure, whether the strict polyphonic principles were followed or the freer compositions prevailed.

R. J. Mayr, Offertorium Improperium 1702

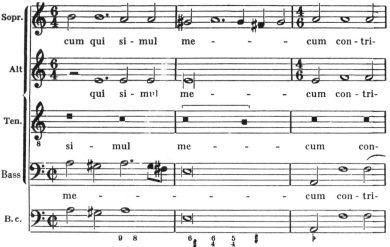

This style utilized the chant in equal note values as *cantus firmus* throughout the piece, writing the notes in Gregorian notation. A chant *cantus* appeared very often in Germany in the seventeenth century in the *stile antico*. Even in the *stile moderno* the chant *cantus firmus* was used on occasion, as well as the *ostinato* bass, canon, etc., to achieve an antiquarian ecclesiastical style.

DEVOTIONAL MUSIC

Although many attempts were made to gain a closer tie with the liturgy, as in *a cappella* music with its links to Gregorian chant, these were the exceptions in an independent musical development that was separating itself from the liturgy more and more.

It was not merely an ignoring of liturgical demands, but rather an exuberance of personal religious experience that introduced songs and instrumental pieces into the service. These included motets in honor of the Blessed Sacrament sung after the Consecration, a sonata at the Offertory, religious songs or instrumental pieces that displaced the chants of the Proper, e.g., flourish or march instead of the Introit, etc. Piety was given the freest rein in the composition of the *cantiones sacrae*. The oratorio form, introduced by St. Philip Neri in company with Animuccia, Anerio and other Roman musicians, provided an outlet both for solo and chorus in the spiritual cantata and the religious oratorio, and in the special forms of the *sepolcro*, the *lamento*, the *meditationes*, the dialog, etc. A new ideal of piety created, in the seventeenth century, its own musical forms.

CHURCH SONGS IN THE VERNACULAR

In line with this we also find an interest in the vernacular hymn, either for solo or chorus, both in church use and as a popular song. In the areas where German was spoken, the early monody of the beginning of the seventeenth century had created German hymns for performance by solo and chorus. In 1623, Friedrich Spee published his first German lieder. It was followed by numerous collections of religious songs set with thorough-bass. In southern Germany, this art was made the vehicle for expressing personal piety by Johannes Khuen (1605–1675), Johannes Werlin (1646), Albert Curtz (1659), and others. In Silesia, Georg Josephus set to music the poetry of Angelus Silesius (Johann Scheffler) in 1657. These songs were distinguished by artistic coloratura work and by folklike simplicity. A portion of this new treasure of songs was adopted as popular church music and thus entered the hymnbooks. These hymns, much like folksongs, appeared in the *Speyrer Gesangbuch* in 1599 and in the hymnal of Mainz in 1605, and gradually obtained more and more space in the *Göttweiher Gesangbuch* of David Gregor Corner (1625), as well as in the hymnals of Cologne and other dioceses. They gained the ascendancy over the dry and often didactic hymns produced by the circle of Michael Vehe and Johann Leisentritt, which were revived in Georg Vogler's catechism hymns of 1625. The German art song combined simple thorough-bass with forms of the aria and orchestral ritornel. This became the predominant form in the secular art song. The song collections of Laurentius von Schnüffi, with their wonderfully baroque titles ("Wondrous Woodland Sounds," 1688; "Marvelous Maypipe," 1692; etc.), were song cycles with instrumental ritornels. Thus from the simple hymn for congregational singing the road led inevitably to the German religious cantata.

Songs in the vernacular also penetrated into the liturgical service, first as a help, or in imitation of the Lutheran service. The Cantual of Mainz (1605) provided for the adoption of German hymns in place of the Proper, and in the closing years of the seventeenth century, German hymns were permitted even in place of the Ordinary. This German "Song-Mass" (*Singmesse*), which is found completely laid out in the hymnals of the early eighteenth century, clearly showed the decline of liturgical choral singing in German-speaking areas and at the same time promoted the further separation of church singing from the liturgy. This estrangement from the liturgy is all the more marked because in the production of the German *Singmesse*, especially in the eighteenth century, congregational singing was combined with that of a choir accompanied by instruments.

In Italy and France the development of the vernacular song was as great, perhaps even greater. This occurred in the dialogs and cantatas, meditations and devotions. In the liturgical service, however, the Latin Gregorian song maintained its leadership, while these other compositions were reserved for extraliturgical devotions. They increasingly helped to accent various aspects of the church year, by means of Passion songs, noëls, etc.

Noël by Piroye 1703

U - nis - sez à nos voix vo - tre douce har-mo - ni - e, an - ges de

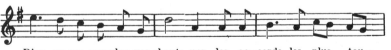

Dieu ne ces - sez plus vos chants, par les ac - cords les plus tou -

chants cé - lébrons cé - lé - brons le di - vin Mes - si - e etc.

The expression of personal emotion had taken the place of the communal attitude of the liturgy.

CHURCH MUSIC IN THE AMERICAS

Eighteenth-century developments in American church music occurred primarily in Latin America and the Spanish colonies of North America. The almost total dependence of the colonial areas on current Spanish musical culture was no longer an advantage, for now there flowed into these areas torrents of the cheap, shallow, orchestrally accompanied repertoire of Europe. No line was drawn between sacred and secular; the *da capo* operatic aria became the model for motets and even for movements of the Mass.

The Spanish missions in the southwestern section of North America, reaching their height around 1800, fared better because of the need for simple music in training the Indian peoples under their tutelage. The California missions in particular flowered at this time, and in 1813 Fray Narcisso Duran (1806–1846), at the Mission San José, published a choirbook consisting mainly of harmonized chants, with a few of the melodies set for two or more parts. Similar books were printed in the Texas, New Mexico and Arizona missions.

The predominance of Protestant culture in the eastern and midwestern sections of the United States affected church music to such an extent that many of the earliest publications in these regions were compiled by non-Catholics such as John Aitken of Philadelphia. Aitken's various compilations were printed between 1787 and 1814, and consisted for the most part of adaptations from secular works. Some Catholic musicians also edited hymnbooks and manuals during this period, including Bishop Cheverus of Boston, who published a volume in 1800 called *Anthems and Hymns Usually Sung in the Catholic Church*. However, even in these few instances the result was an ever greater stockpile of mediocre, saccharine music.

What is particularly noticeable, whether the music stems from Catholic or non-Catholic hands, is its total secularization. The Catholic colonists in those parts of the New World which became the United States brought with them little or no musical culture; they had scarcely any liturgical tradition, so that a secularized musical ideal was inevitable upon contact with the non-Catholic population. Since the scattered congregations continued to have the character of missions, there was little chance for the cultivation of a church music that differed from that of the surrounding areas. It was not till the advent of monastic foundations and the introduction of the parochial school system that any progress was made.

CHURCH MUSIC AS AN ORNAMENT OF WORSHIP

The multiplicity of forms of church music in the seventeenth century and the search for a personal expression are indicative of an attitude, changed basically since the period of classical polyphony. Church music was considered as an ornament of worship, and a means for providing artistic display ; no longer was it looked upon as a liturgical unit. The notion that church music is an integral part of the liturgy was lost. Baroque worship and musical conception had overstepped the balance of form and setting of the sixteenth century by this external embellishment and thus transferred the center of gravity. No longer was the liturgical action itself the focal point ; instead it was man, and music was conceived of in terms of its effect on man, and in reference to man's taste. Temporal and spatial distinctions came to the fore and the objective communal attitude of a music *of* worship was replaced by music *at* worship that unfolded freely and without restraint.

This conception was given outward expression by moving the musical choir to the back of the church, as provided in baroque buildings, in contrast to the earlier position of the liturgical singing choir near the altar. The use of women's voices and orchestras in church since the seventeenth century took church music still further from its liturgical task. Another reason for this rupture came because the priest no longer confined himself, as in the early Middle Ages, to the prayers or songs assigned to him but now said all the liturgical texts as in a *Missa privata*, even when they were sung by the choir. The sense of liturgy so deteriorated that the liturgical text to be sung was disregarded, shortened or even replaced as the need arose.

CHANGE IN CHURCH MUSIC LIFE

At the same time the changes in the general musical environment left their traces on music for the church. The courtly musical life of the seventeenth century adopted its own peculiar forms. Princely courts, large and small, became centers of musical life, but in the country at large music lost some of its importance. In the same way church music flourished in the cathedrals, in the court churches of ecclesiastical and secular princes who cultivated music within their chapels, and in the large monastic churches and places of pilgrimage. Elsewhere church music declined. In the sixteenth century the lead in church music was taken by schools and choir schools, but the new works of church music presented demands that could not be met by the schools, especially as their musical culture declined. Parishes in general were in no position to maintain soloists, chorus and orchestra. They had to restrict themselves to simple functional music. Gregorian chant, revised and accompanied according to contemporary standards, was the work of choirs that did not always distinguish themselves artistically. For "figured music," in addition to the usual paid singers, male and female, other vocalists and instrumentalists were engaged, especially on feast days. The distinctive character of the liturgical church choir thus disappeared. The laicizing of the church choir was therefore another step in the separation of church music from its proper liturgical attitude, a further step in its secularization.

CHAPTER 13

Church Music
Shaped by the Emotions

FREE MUSICAL DEVELOPMENT

The emphasis on personal piety in prayer during the baroque era contrasted with the official, liturgical prayer of the church. Musical composition was broadened to include this new attitude, but at the same time,
functional music for the liturgy continued to be written, although it was
influenced by the new trends and considerably adapted to popular tastes.
Gregorian chant and the *stile antico* were still cultivated and in them a
link with the demands of worship was maintained. However, by the
year 1700, the unity between church music and the liturgy, as it existed
in the Middle Ages and to some extent in the sixteenth century, was no
longer a reality. By the beginning of the eighteenth century, the rationalistic "art for art's sake," which had penetrated every aspect of musical
life, had embraced church music also.

With the beginning of the seventeenth century, this very personal piety
in prayer gained expression in many musical devices. This was true
especially in those places where the dominant type of church music had
been freed from ties with the liturgy. This promoted a variety of often
opposing developments. The foundation of this church music was personal
religious experience, not the effort to combine this personal attitude of
religious expression with the demands of worship. In the forms of expression it employed, this art considered itself free from traditions and from
liturgical ties. Similarly, it disregarded the temporal limitations set by
the liturgy.

136

The independence of the *stile moderno*, and the constant effort to shape new expressional forms unhampered by tradition, hastened its development and ended any possible link with older stylistic media. This brought about a change: whereas the seventeenth century strove for a compromise between the *stile antico* and the *stile moderno*, in eighteenth-century church music the two styles separated widely. This resulted in further independent evolution of the *stile moderno*, and strict, often lifeless, composition in the *stile antico*. The *stile misto* lost its importance, although even in the eighteenth century the two styles were sometimes used alternately in small sections within a composition for their expressive value.

NEW STYLISTIC FORMS OF THE NEAPOLITANS

The center of the new development was Naples where not only church music but the opera, the cantata, and the oratorio were influenced by this new form of expression. The core of this form was melodic expression; to it even the text was subordinated, with a total disregard for grammar and verbal accent. Once the text lost its dominant position, a purely musical principle of organization took over. Melodies were determined by the length of the phrase or period and by the meter employed, while the harmony depended on the cadence.

The first statement of the principles of the Neopolitan *stile moderno* was undertaken by Carissimi's pupil, Alessandro Scarlatti (1659–1725), and his circle. Leonardo Leo (1694–1744), Francesco Durante (1684–1755), Gaetano Greco (c. 1680), Nicolo Fago (1674–1745), Giovanni Battista Pergolesi (1710–1736), Niccolo Porpora (1686–1766), Leonardo Vinci (1690–1730), and others produced a purely musical type of expression in church music on the basis of a personal interpretation of the sense and sound of the text, but to the neglect of its grammatical and accentual formation.

F. Durante, Magnificat 1746

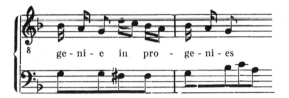

Contrast and expressiveness in both melody and harmony characterized this art. It was used for choral settings and for solo works, but in both the emotional factor was foremost. This style set the pattern for composition in various countries, where it was always called the "Italian style." It brought about a refinement of the media of expression created in the seventeenth century and emphasized vocal and instrumental solo composition. Chorus and orchestra were also influenced. The earlier system of contrasting the families of instruments by means of concerto-ripieno sections gave way to a new emphasis on the strings in contrast to solo wind instruments. While formerly two violins, bass, and *basso continuo* alternated with three violas or three trombones, Scarlatti and his circle combined the strings into one unit, dropping the old concerto-ripieno technique. This was true of church music as well as of the opera. It was a complete departure from *colla parte* and ritornel writing in favor of an independent accompaniment only loosely connected with the singing voices.

The chief interest of this art lay in the melody which was an extended cantilena filled with coloratura pasages both in vocal and in instrumental writing. The aria (A-B and A-B-A) was the chief form employed. Contrast was still achieved by solo-tutti and concerto-ripieno techniques, but with the expanded melodic treatment afforded by the aria, with its emphasis on expressiveness, the alternating of arioso and recitative passages contributed greatly to this desired contrast. However, this resulted in a broad cleavage between the liturgical text and the musical form, for the latter was employed with complete disregard of the liturgical requirements of the text. This juxtaposition of recitative and arioso passages helped to heighten the emotional expression of certain sections of the text, for this art had for its purpose the presentation of an overall interpretation of the text rather than the characterization of each word. This emotional effect could be achieved only by employing the devices and techniques of the period, which were found commonly in instrumental music and in opera. To characterize Neopolitan church music as "opera in church" fails to recognize that the emotional expression which church music was striving for could only be achieved by means of contemporary techniques, even though they were also employed in operatic composition.

The biggest problem of the new artistic attitude involved the chorus, which was essential to church music but quite infrequent in Neopolitan opera. This choral work utilized both melodic and recitative-declamatory principles, with the result that it was used most frequently in homophonic and cadential settings. Sections here and there were developed in the *stile antico* as fugal work. Sometimes contrapuntal techniques were combined with *concertante* themes. This choral style employed orchestral accompaniment or only a *basso continuo* which the Neopolitans frequently performed on the organ. In combination with instruments the choir's function became that of merely filling out the chords of the

Mass by L. Leo

harmony in a declamatory style. When writing in the *stile antico* was attempted with instrumental accompaniment, the orchestra played either *colla parte* or elaborated the voice parts.

The greatest opportunity for choral writing occurred with the closing fugue on "Amen." This gave a fitting expression to the jubilant pulsation of the Gloria. It was an all encompassing emotional force.

THE A CAPPELLA STYLE OF THE NEAPOLITANS

The church music of the Neapolitan school represented an extreme advance into a new sphere of musical art filled with pathos, sentimentality, and an exaggeration of personal emotion. But because this *stile moderno* often passed beyond the limits of what was liturgically fitting, the com-

A. Scarlatti, Mass for 5 voices

posers who employed it were frequently led to cultivate also the strict *stile antico*. Alessandro Scarlatti, Leonardo Leo and other Neapolitan composers attempted what was for that period strict composition in the *stile antico*. Although they imitated the classic polyphony as closely as they could, contemporary devices influenced them in their treatment of melody, harmonic tension and cadences. That the Neapolitans wrote in the *stile antico* shows that the polyphony of the sixteenth century had come to be regarded as the official ecclesiastical style, and that those who used the *stile moderno* were aware of this ecclesiastical type of expression. The *stile moderno*, like the *stile antico*, found its own development and its own sphere of expression. The *stile antico* was used especially in Advent and Lent, giving the *a cappella* masses the designation *Missae quadragesimales*. This contributed to the idea that it was a style of sorrow and seriousness.

Toward the end of the century inventiveness and expressive strength began to ebb and the forms became mere mannerisms. With composers like Nicolo Sala (1720–1800), who in his *Regole del contrappunto* (1794) once more summarized the strict style, and Giacomo Tritta (1733–1824), and especially the prolific Niccolo Antonio Zingarelli (1752–1837), church music among the Neapolitans finally disintegrated.

THE CHURCH'S ATTITUDE TOWARD THE NEW ART

The impact of the Neapolitans on the formation of a new expression in church music was bound to have a profound influence on church music everywhere. Like every innovation affecting liturgy, it occasioned an ecclesiastical decision in its regard. In 1749, Pope Benedict XIV in his encyclical *Annus qui* stated the position of the Church. In 1600, Clement VIII, in the *Caeremoniale episcoporum*, settled the question of the use of the organ in divine service. Alexander VII (1657), Innocent XI (1678), and Innocent XII (1692) condemned the abuses in the new art but recognized its serious development. Benedict XIV, on the same principles, granted recognition to the new contemporary style with its instrumental accompaniment and sanctioned purely instrumental pieces, provided they avoided a theatrical expression. These decrees said nothing about the problems of composition or the manner of performance, and no reference was made to the medieval liturgical melodies as essential to church music. In keeping with the times, emphasis was put on the mood of the music: "the feeling of piety." This opened up the possibility for many interpretations, and specific prescriptions soon had to be published regarding the completeness and the choice of texts. Here ecclesiastical authority was able to establish something more definite than it could in regard to the musical media of expression. Musicians were instructed that voices and instruments should work together "to arouse the sentiments of the faithful, so that they may be the more joyfully excited to piety and devotion." In this basic legislation of 1749 the rule and measure were not the demands of the liturgy but the mood and attitude of the faithful. Thus even ecclesiastical authority reflected contemporary views and departed from medieval inflexibility. The intelligibility of the words was emphasized, giving a basis for the restriction of instruments, but the essence of the instruction was the ecclesiastical character and religious mood of the music in contrast to that of a worldly and theatrical character. Thus the ecclesiastical authority adopted as the principle for evaluating church music the effect of the musician's art on the worshiper rather than the demands of the liturgical action itself.

The course of further development followed this individualistic, personal interpretation of the relationship of music to worship. Local customs and personal tastes were recognized, and since the Council of Trent had left decisions in matters of music to the local bishops, the regional character of viewpoints on church music was already admitted. But with the decrees of the eighteenth century, the Church definitely opened the way to this individualistic art. Thus national schools and viewpoints as well as local tastes and fashions could unfold in church music without hindrance. The only limits on this purely musical development were the liturgical texts, certain fixed forms for the service, and the various festal seasons.

Because of the prohibition of musical instruments, the *stile antico* had an external reason for existence. In addition, it was the accepted method for the study of musical theory and composition nearly everywhere, although its use as a teaching device in many instances obscured its original purpose and many of its fine points. The examination compositions of the Accademia Filarmonica in Bologna, which was the most important center for the promotion of the strict scholastic style of counterpoint since the middle of the eighteenth century, show how during the last decades of that century contrapuntal work had declined as a serious art, and how the strict style, fostered until the time of Padre Martini, had given way to the light contemporary style.

CHURCH MUSIC AMONG THE VENETIANS

The stress on the expression of personal piety and on the tastes of the congregation resulted in distinct stylistic groups. Sentimentality, with its foundations in rationalism and the Enlightenment, had in the course of the eighteenth century produced a peculiar attitude toward art. Sentimentality prevented an objective interpretation of liturgy or a common style of piety, although this attitude was to some degree associated with tradition. In Italy each area found its own solution to the problem of combining the new sentiment with an expression truly ecclesiastical. As in Naples, Roman and Venetian circles, and the numerous schools of upper Italy, had their own solutions, more or less similar to that of Naples.

Following the principles of Giovanni Gabrieli, Claudio Monteverdi, Marc Antonio Cesti and Giovanni Legrenzi, Venetian musicians continued the *concertante* style in combination with contrapuntal voice leading and the use of chorus. Antonio Caldara (1670–1736) gained expression in his church music by means of a delicate interweaving of voices. Francesco Antonio Calegari, Marc Antonio Ziani, and others, using these *cantabile* melodies, created music that met the contemporary taste and at the same time observed the distinction between worldly and ecclesiastical expression. A second center of this Venetian circle of composers grew up in Vienna, where Venetian masters had directed church music and the opera since the early seventeenth century. The external development of the tonal resources continued to be the predominant trait of this style all through the eighteenth century. But besides the solo work, the choral setting was especially cultivated. The chorus, even in the *stile moderno*, was not restricted to a mere chordal composition, as in the Neapolitan circle. How much the Venetians in their church music were interested in the chorus is shown by the remark of Antonio Lotti (1667–1740), that "the true art of composition is found only in Germany" where, among the cantors, strict counterpoint was being promoted. Lotti himself especially cultivated the *stile antico* in his church music, but even when he used the *stile moderno* he sought to enrich free melodic lines with contrapuntal depth. The basically dramatic character of his church music gave special value to his principles of composition. His choice of few or many voices, of solo or chorus, was made to serve the purposes of dramatic expression as well as of mood. His compositions obtained an increase of inner tension and motion by means of chromatic turns of melody and altered chords. The tradition of contrapuntal composition was really stronger in such works of the ecclesiastical *stile moderno* than in the solo art of the Neapolitans with its emphasis on melody.

THE CHURCH MUSIC OF UPPER ITALY

In the church-music centers of northern Italy the ruling problem was the same — the complementing of the choral composition with the new techniques of expression. In continuing the tradition of Maurizio Cazzati and Giovanni Paolo Colonna, musicians at Bologna took a leading role. The Accademia Filarmonica was founded by Vincenzo Maria Carrati in 1666. Giacomo Antonio Perti (1661–1756), his pupil, Padre Martini (1706–1784), and others influenced the course of church music in their period not only by their own compositions but especially by the work of their school. The basis of their art was the strict contrapuntal style which they gave a new theoretical presentation.

Padre Martini (*Saggio di Contrappunto*, 1774), Giuseppe Paolucci (*Arte prattica di Contrappunto*, 3 vols., 1765), and others described the strict *stile antico* from which they drew their principles of a *stile moderno* for church music. Padre Martini's *Mass in D Minor* (1734) for orchestra, written entirely in canon, is a demonstration of his extraordinary craftsmanship and at the same time an indication of the constructive art which produced such works. He endeavored to give the *stile moderno*, with its broken chords, runs, ornaments and cantabile settings, a certain depth by means of his contrapuntal devices, but it must be granted that he frequently achieved only the mere structural externals. This stylistic confusion and uncertainty was entirely overcome by Martini's pupil, Paolucci (1726–1776), in his clear exposition of the stylistic peculiarities of the Palestrinan style as seen in his *Arte prattica di Contrappunto*. The choice of examples, as well as his exercises, show that he grasped the stylistic essence of the *stile antico* with an understanding unique for his time.

Padua was a center for church-music development in northern Italy, where the tradition of Constanzo Porta, Antonio Calegari, and others was continued especially by Padre Martini's friend, Padre Francesco Vallotti (1697–1780). For ecclesiastical expression he used both the *stile antico* and the *stile moderno*. Vallotti is also important as a theorist.

In Loretto, the church-music field was dominated by Andrea Basili, one of the most prolific Italian composers of the eighteenth century, who constructed his compositions in strict counterpoint. He differed sharply from his son Francesco (1767–1850), whose church music was dominated by the sentimental fashions of the period. Andrea was many-sided in the setting of his church compositions and in the forms and media he employed. Harmonic tensions helped to strengthen the movement of his settings.

Mass for Male Choir by A. Basili

In Lucca, where the tradition of the great motets (*motettone*) on the feast of the Holy Cross brought musicians together from near and far, church music in both the old and the new style flourished especially under the ancestors of the great opera composer Giacomo Puccini (1858–1924): Giacomo (1712–1781), Antonio (1747–1832), and Domenico (1771–1815).

Everywhere in northern Italy the same effort to strengthen the old and the new style by means of contrapuntal work could be noticed. Although solo-coloratura was not missing here, it was not given the mobility of melodic form found among the Neapolitans. The shallowness of melodic expression, as well as of form and harmonic setting found at Naples during the last decades of the eighteenth century, influenced the church music of northern Italy and destroyed the peculiar stamp which that music had before 1780.

THE STRICT CHORAL STYLE IN ROME

In marked contrast to the free development of church music among the Neapolitans was the continuation of the choral and ornamental style in Rome during the eighteenth century. Giuseppe Ottavio Pitoni (1657–1743) wrote a large number of church-music compositions ranging from 2 to 48 voices, which expanded upon the choral processes of ancient polyphony, although he held firm to the stylistic features of the *stile antico*.

Short themes and a harmonic foundation for their contrapuntal treatment are characteristic of this new appearance of the old polyphonic style.

Because the papal chapel refused to admit the organ and other instruments, the *a cappella* style continued to be cultivated all through the eighteenth century. The quest for fullness of tone was met by the multiplication of voices, Gregorio Ballabene (1720–1803) writing a forty-eight-voice mass. Multiplication of choirs played a large role in the crea-

G. O. Pitoni

tions of Pietro Guglielmi (1727–1804), Giuseppe Jannacconi (1741–1816), and others. In marked contrast, Pietro Paolo Bencini, Giovanni Battista Costanzi (✠1778), Giovanni Battista Casali (1715–1792) and others used the old and new styles side by side, and even mixed traces of the suppleness and sonority of the *stile moderno* with the strict style

Motet by A. Bencini, 1735

(e.g., by using a broken-chord melisma). Pasquale Pisari (1725–1778)
stands out as a close follower of the ancient style. It was with justice that
Padre Martini called him the Palestrina of the eighteenth century. The
greatest part of his church music is written in the strict *a cappella* style.
He often employed voice leading in his *a cappella* settings.

Pisari, Psalm (Double canon at the fifth)

The compact choral setting is also the center of interest for the Roman composers in their church music with orchestral accompaniment in the *stile moderno*; this distinguished them from the Neapolitans. In the arrangement of Palestrina's masses for choir and orchestra by Girolamo Chiti (✝1759), the conception of the choir is quite different from that of the Neapolitan composers with their harmonic declamations. But in Chiti's own works in the old style the chordal arrangement of the voices determined the tonal effect in spite of the contrapuntal leading of voices.

G. Chiti, Missa Fuge dilecte mi

CHURCH MUSIC IN FRANCE

In France as in Rome strict choral work continued to be the heart of church music creation. The quarrel between the followers of Gluck and those of Puccini over Italian influence in opera had a similar counterpart in church music, as the French tended to object to the Italian style. The declamatory style of Jean Baptiste Lully and his circle continued to be followed, although Italian innovations modified it somewhat in the works of Marc Antoine Charpentier (1634–1704), André Cardinal Destouches (1669–1749), Nicolas Bernier (1664–1734), Michel Richard de Lalande

(1657–1726), André Campra (1660–1744), and others. What determined the peculiar development of church music in France at this time was the well arranged ornamentation and declamation which excluded both the recitative and a free development of the melody. The prominence of the low mass with solemnity in place of the liturgical high mass, since the closing years of the seventeenth century, encouraged the creation of motets, psalms and church cantatas rather than liturgical music. Following the tradition of the seventeenth century, organ music continued to hold the center of interest for French composers all through the eighteenth century. Gregorian themes continued to be the bases for the organ masses and liturgical organ compositions of François Couperin, Louis Nicholas Clerembault (1676–1749), Nicolas de Grigny (c. 1671–1703), Michel Corette (1709–1795), and others, although they tended to transform and abandon even the old contrapuntal handling of the organ setting.

CHURCH MUSIC IN GERMANY

In the art of Johann Sebastian Bach (1685–1750) in the first half of the eighteenth century, Germany achieved the apex of a new kind of contrapuntal art. The strict tradition of north German cantors had, by its conservatism, set up a barrier in Protestant Germany against the invasion of the unrestrained Italian emotional and sentimental art. This restraining barrier was decisive for the development of Lutheran church music. But even in the Catholic centers of Germany the Italian *concertante* church style was not adopted to the same degree as in Naples. One reason for retaining the stricter forms was the close ties of the German courts with France, many musicians being sent to Paris for training. Another reason was the local tradition which would not depart from the strict counterpoint even in the newer art. The work of Ercole and Giuseppe Bernabei (1620–1687; 1649–1732) and of Johann Kaspar Kerll (1627–1693) continued to a great extent to have influence in Bavaria in the first half of the eighteenth century. In Vienna Johann Joseph Fux (c. 1660–1741) taught the strict style of composition in his *Gradus ad Parnassum* (1725). He used the *a cappella* style but evaluated from his own viewpoint, which emphasized emotion, harmonic ties and careful metrical arrangement. He also employed an expressive style with contemporary orchestral accompaniment, as well as a mixture of both techniques in the same compositions "since sometimes one, two, three or more voices concertize with the instruments, and sometimes the full chorus does." Although his numerous church compositions seldom conformed to the ideals he set up theoretically, chiefly because of his inventive aridity, his influence on church music in the eighteenth century was extraordinary. All textbooks on musical composition even up to our own day were based on his theory and most German musicians in the eighteenth century studied music theory according to his method.

In Vienna, where the Italian influence was very strong ever since the time of the Venetians, there were some Italians who followed the strict style, Marc Antonio Ziani or Matteo Pallotta (1689–1748). George Christoph Wagenseil (1715–1777) and Georg Pasterwitz (1730–1803) became masters of church composition in the strict *stile antico*.

Chr. Wagenseil, Improperium

The composers who followed this direction and cultivated the *stile antico* along with new orchestral forms were numerous. In Bohemia, Bohguslav Czernohorsky, Joseph Ferdinand Seegert (1716–1782) and Franz Tuma (1701–1774) contributed significantly by their strict work in this style. Franz Xaver Brixi (1732–1771), F. Christoph Neubauer (1760–1795), Franz Xaver Richter (1709–1789), and Jiri Antonin

Benda (1722–1795), and others, although they searched for new means of expression with every device available, retained strict counterpoint especially in *a cappella* pieces. In Dresden, direct ties with the new Italian church music existed through the works of Antonio Lotti (1667–1740), Giovanni Ristori (1692–1753) and Johann Adolf Hasse (1699–1783), and these in turn had a marked influence on Johann David Heinichen (1683–1729), Johann D. Zelenka (1679–1745), Johann Gottlieb Naumann (1741–1801) and Franz Seydelmann (1748–1806).

Johann Joseph Fux found an earnest successor in Johann Georg Albrechtsberger (1736–1809), who continued teaching the strict style of composition and handed it on to a new generation of musicians. He regarded polyphonic church music as the acme; the fugue was described as "the most necessary species of church music." In his *Gründliche Anweisung zur Komposition* (1790), Albrechtsberger collected all the teaching on the strict style in the very period when the Viennese classical composers were writing music far removed from the *stile antico*.

Along with this group of Viennese theoreticians the Benedictine Meinrad Spiess (1683–1761), in southern Germany, worked to bridge the gap between the strict church style and the "galant" style. In Germany, because strict contrapuntal composition was cultivated both in the *stile antico* and the *stile moderno*, the courtly galant style with its sentimental expression was not widely fostered. However, Marianus Königsberger (1708–1769) and many other composers were forced by their positions to follow the trend of the times; in their works artistic seriousness was lost along with liturgical integrity.

Gregorian chant found little place in the divine service. If used at all, it was arbitrarily refashioned to conform to the taste of the times. Everywhere efforts were made to simplify the chant or to create weak imitations of it, in order to halt its decline. Its artistic performance had already reached a low ebb in the seventeenth century. The church choir surrendered its performance to special choristers. Frequently the Gregorian chants were replaced in the service by compositions on freely selected texts or by instrumental pieces, or they were even left out entirely to make room for the massive figures with orchestral accompaniment.

CHAPTER 14

Symphonic Church Music

EFFORTS TO ACHIEVE EXPRESSIVENESS

If in the first half of the eighteenth century church musicians directed their efforts toward expressing emotion by contrasting sections in the concerto and sonata forms, in the second half of that century they sought a greater unity in their compositions. In instrumental music the "Mannheim School" displayed these unifying efforts most strongly. The orchestral crescendo, which avoids sharp contrasts in dynamics by bridging the difference between sections through the use of a gradual increase or decrease of intensity, was as much a sign of the new expressive attitude of a sentimental art as was the elaboration of themes or the development of the sonata or the symphony. In instrumental music this effort for expressiveness found its fulfillment in the Viennese classical school.

Following the trend of the times, church music utilized this expressiveness in order to awaken common religious sentiments. However, in this effort the liturgical purpose of church music was lost sight of. This was true with respect to chant as well as in setting texts to new music. Composers did not follow the organization and construction of the text, but rather concerned themselves only with the demands of the musical forms. This accounts for the practice of including the intonations of the Gloria and the Credo within the composition, as well as the popularity of the pastoral mass where the liturgical text was joined to music of an extraliturgical, individual and sentimental nature. The repetition of words for the sake of emphasis (e.g., *non, credo*) was a result partly of this in-

154

dividualistic expressiveness and partly of purely musical and metrical considerations (e.g., *et in terra pax / pax hominibus*). This expressiveness, determined as it was by a rationalistic construction and by sentimentalism, sought for thematic contrast and its elaboration in the closed symphonic form. Thus the ecclesiastical vocal style borrowed techniques from instrumental music.

SEPARATION OF NEAPOLITAN CHURCH MUSIC FROM THE LITURGY

In Naples the second generation of composers at first continued the *stile moderno* and the *stile antico* and, for special interpretative effect, even used them side by side in short sections. The stressing of weak linear and harmonic activity promoted motion in thirds, the use of altered harmonies and the extension of the voices by the addition of a second soprano. Recitative and aria became frequent as solo forms. This church-music style, elaborating on the work of Francesco Durante, was fostered in the compositions of Niccolo Jomelli (1714–1774), Gaetano Latilla (1711–1791), Carlo Cotumacci (1698–1775), Giovanni Paisiello (1741–1816), and others. In their hands church music went to the extremes of sentimentality and dramatic pathos. In the second half of the eighteenth century the old baroque *concertante* style disappeared, and the old cantata form was influenced by the symphonic device of thorough-composition. A new form of composition arose in the so-called "number masses," where sections of the text were composed symphonically as separate and complete pieces. Composers who had made a name for themselves in opera and instrumental music like Tommaso Traetta (1727–1779), Davide Perez (1711–1778), Antonio Maria Gasparo Sacchini (1734–1786), Niccolo Jomelli (1714–1774), and Giovanni Paisiello wrote this type of church music. Ambrogio Minoja (1752–1825), Baldassare Galuppi (1706–1785), and many others at the various centers of Italian church music continued these attempts to build on the foundation of the cantata.

Instrumental writing set the pattern for vocal compositions, whether they were accompanied by instruments or merely by a thorough-bass.

Thus a new vocal form for church music came into being, novel in the devices it used for expression and lacking the independent movement of voices of the ancient polyphony. Like the chamber cantata, this new organ-accompanied church music utilized the *bel canto*. The widespread

Domenico Cimarosa, Mass

Anfossi, Mass for Four Voices (Christe)

form of organ mass, which included solo organ interludes alongside chordal organ accompaniments, had its basis here as well as in the *a cappella* mass with its *basso continuo* accompaniment.

The seriousness that was natural to true church music was far removed from such a form. It followed the purely musical principles of creativeness found in the court style of the period.

This estrangement from the liturgy resulted in settings that were based on a musical foundation only, completely disregarding liturgical principles. The most outrageous example of this was the "Kyrie–Gloria" type of mass, in which these two parts were composed in so lengthy a fashion that the other parts of the Ordinary were omitted. This upset

Andantino   Mass for Three Voices, with Organ, by A. Aimone

the equilibrium of the divine service. Either the remainder was done in
chant or the Mass was continued as a low Mass or as one said independently during the performance of the "concert" in the choir-loft. The
"art for art's sake" conception of church music, as well as the rationalistic attitude toward divine service, led to this complete severance of
church music from its liturgical foundation.

CHURCH MUSIC DURING THE ENLIGHTENMENT
IN GERMANY

In Italy, because of the development of the *bel canto*, vocal techniques
took precedence over the instrumental, but in Germany the lead was
taken by the instrumental symphonic manner of composition. The Mannheim composers, with their new treatment of the orchestra, and especially
with their emphasis on themes, started trends for ecclesiastical solo and
choral composition that soon had far-reaching effects. Of all the Mann-

heim composers, Franz X. Richter (1709–1789) was most dedicated to church music. Ignaz Holzbauer (1711–1783) also wrote for church, and his German *Singmesse*, like his Latin masses, adopted the grand forms of the symphonic style and presented an emotional and dramatic interpretation of the text.

Of the Mannheim circle, however, it was George Vogler (1749–1814) who both by his compositions and his theoretical writings had the greatest

Holzbauer, German Mass

influence on church music. Rationalism and romantic feelings gave his church music a double focus. Dramatic effort brought about a thoroughly individualistic creativity that sought constantly for novel forms. Through his activity as the teacher of numerous musicians and through his critical works, his ideas were spread far and wide and given an attention they did not deserve, since they were largely personal and hardly reflected the viewpoint of the period. In Vogler's compositions sections of serious writing are mixed with others that are purely formal, as in the bass solo in the Sanctus of his first *Missa solemnis.*

Sanc - tus, sanc-tus, sanc - tus, sanc-tus,

sanc - tus Do - mi-nus De - us Sa - ba - oth

In southern Germany this art was adopted and developed by Johann Zach (1699–1773), Joseph Martin Kraus (1756–1792), Placidus von Camerloher (1718–1782), Joseph Riepl (1708–1782), and many pseudo-composers who lacked not only the requisite liturgical and artistic taste but even the very groundwork of musical technique. They completely debased the church music to be used by their "country choirs" and thus severed it from all serious development.

A small but typical example of this kind of church music written by literally hundreds of these musicians, both lay and cleric, in the late eighteenth century, is this excerpt from the third mass of the *Eight Masses,* Opus 1, of Lambert Kraus (1728–1790) :

cu - jus re - gni   re - gni non,   non,   non,

non,   non,   non,   non,   non,   non,

non,   non,   non   e - rit   fi - nis,   non

non,   non,   non   e - rit   fi - nis,   non

The church aria and the German masses and vespers suffered the same fate as the Latin church music, a disintegration of the ecclesiastical style in reference to melody, harmony, technique of composition, declamation, meter, rhythm and tonal concepts. A favorite practice was to set a well-known popular melody to an ecclesiastical text. Thus in 1795 an anonymous "Lover of Church Music" published a collection entitled *XII Ariae seu Offertoria* in which the author arranges favorite operetta tunes of Ditter von Dittersdorf (1739–1799) with "Latin texts fitted to the sacred actions of the church and the solemn service of God, because he considered these the most proper. For this purpose he chose those texts which not only suited the meter of the original text, but also were capable of expressing the feeling that dominated the text and of supporting and inspiring religious devotion."

As in the sixteenth century, parody again became widespread at the end of the eighteenth and the beginning of the nineteenth century. Instrumental compositions by Haydn, Mozart, Beethoven, Schubert, Weber and others were set to ecclesiastical texts and published as church music. The popularity of transcriptions and variations spread to the field of church music as well, where arrangements and revisions are found in numberless editions. Title pages at the turn of the century indicate that the works were intended for "country and cathedral choirs," ranging from the simplest setting for one and two voices and organ to a grand production with soli, chorus and orchestra. The "customer" had to be just as enticed by the advertising of the music as he had to be considered in creating it.

This attitude of the Enlightenment, with its roots sunk in Josephinism, meant the alienation of church music from the liturgy and therefore from its own real purpose and essence. Church music could reach its goal only in a world of artistic and liturgical thought rooted in popular devotion. But the age of the Enlightenment itself had rendered impossible any artistic elevation of existing traditions in the courts and musical centers. Any liturgical conception that would embrace church-music life as a whole, from the smallest village church to the largest cathedral, became impossible because the Enlightenment had destroyed the foundations of liturgy in the world and in the church, in the monastery and in the rectory. The only thing that could bring about a change was a basic and general reform of ecclesiastical life, which would include church music too. For such a reform, however, the eighteenth century was not ripe.

CHURCH MUSIC OF THE VIENNESE CLASSICISTS

Because of the lead taken by German music in the closing years of the eighteenth century, Neapolitan fashions and techniques were introduced in every area of church-music activity. As the Viennese classicists reached the zenith of their creative activity, they wrote church music also, giving it artistic depth. But their basic principle of composition was not the delineation of a mood in individual sections as found in the number-compositions of Neapolitan church music, but an independent development based on contrasting themes. This gradually changed from a free musical formation to a clearer textual expression. Thus symphonic art and its thematic activity joined forces with vocal music. Church music abandoned its connection with the cantata, opera and oratorio and took up instead the now dominant form of symphonic music. This change was at first quite timid, with the old forms retained but penetrated by the new thematic treatment. In the earlier masses of Haydn and Mozart this search for new creative forms is apparent, but it was not until the later church music of these masters, as well as Beethoven and Schubert, that symphonic-thematic work became the dominating principle.

Wolfgang Amadeus Mozart's (1756–1791) church music first unfolded in the arioso-cantata style, but in the city of Salzburg practical considerations of a local nature modified his style to some extent. His inexhaustible power of imagination and utterance freed his compositions from mere mannerism and formality, and this accounts for the wealth of form and expression in his masses, litanies, motets and vespers. Sections that are

richly expressive are occasionally found side by side with material that
has little to say, but in the end his own ability came more determinately
to the fore, to create works with depth like his *Ave verum* (1791) and the
Requiem (1791).

If in his *Missa brevis in G Major* (1768) Mozart still adhered to models
of his own age, in the two masses written the following year, the *D Minor*
and *C Major*, he arrived at a new style and form. The courtly and almost
playful attitude of Mozart's church music achieves symphonic unity independently of the text. Even in his early works he produced parts that are
quite expressive, not in the sense of liturgical empathy but as the utterance of an untrammeled imagination. However, his incomplete *Mass in C
Minor* (1782–3) gave his church music a new orientation. This Bach-like
and Handel-like art had acquired, in contrapuntal work, an expressiveness
truly ecclesiastical.

In his *Requiem*, Mozart fashioned a work of religious expression with
contrapuntal devices and also an intensification of expression in the solo
sections. He combined in this work the techniques of the Viennese classicists with the severe expressive art of Bach and Handel.

Joseph Haydn (1732–1809), even more than Mozart, approached a true
church music through the intensity of his artistic expression. Even in his
early compositions he had overcome the limitations of the cantata style
by his contrapuntal work and compressed the free solo development into
a contrapuntal solo ensemble. The masses written after 1796 offered
personal forms of expression which were characterized especially by the
increase in the use of contrapuntal material, thematic work in the sym-

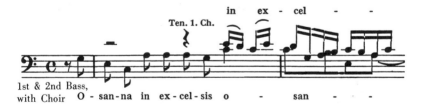

For Orchestra and Voices

phonic style, and the substitution of the quartet-choir technique for the solo-tutti practice of the cantata. Haydn was able to transcend the forms of his time. If in certain trends he did adhere to traditional concepts and forms (final fugues, martial music before *Dona nobis pacem*, etc.), he transformed many of these traditional techniques and made them the unique expression of his own ideas. It is from this personal conception of church music that one can explain the serene traits in Haydn's music as indications of his untroubled religious sensibility.

Ludwig van Beethoven, (1770–1827) expanded the church music of Haydn in his *Missa solemnis*. As early as his *Mass in C Major* (1807) the power that shaped the music was his religious feeling, which was not the unquestioning joy of Haydn, but a ringing profession of faith. This work still remained within the restricted limits of the divine service, but the *Missa solemnis* burst all the limitations of the usual forms and became a personal expression that was bound to overcome all external restrictions. The magnitude of his interpretation of the text and his artistic setting of it gave Beethoven's *Missa* a unique position. It broadened the mass into symphonic forms and, although it was composed for the enthronement ceremony of Archduke Rudolph as bishop of Olmütz in 1820, the mass abandoned all strictly liturgical demands. This artistic expansion of church music led to a complete disregard of the music's usefulness for the service. At the same time it led to the music's becoming independent religious expression, freed from ecclesiastical restrictions. Personal art triumphed over ecclesiastical and liturgical considerations.

These tendencies continued as the emphasis on feeling, so characteristic of Romanticism, encouraged the display of personal attitudes without regard for possible alienation from liturgical propriety, under the influence of a subjectively conceived ideal. The works of Franz Schubert (1797–1828) are characterized by a lyricism that contrasts with the dramatic efforts of Karl Maria von Weber. The use of harmonic colors, characteristic motifs, and extension of form were traits of this art. In his great *A Flat Major* (1822) and *E Flat Major* (1828) masses, Schubert created works of profound expressiveness. The arioso-solo art was repressed, following the example of Mozart; and alternation of ensemble and choir in the manner of Haydn became the focal point. Fugal work played a prominent role, with a delicate use of harmony and declamation. Although the liturgical text was often treated very freely and at times without understanding, the masterful shaping of mood gave Schubert's church music a character that was truly meaningful. His lesser works, like the *G Major Mass* (1815) or the German *Singmesse*, are distinguished by their lyric tenderness and delicate feeling.

The dramatic element in the music of Karl Maria von Weber (1786–

1826) is in striking contrast to the lyricism of Schubert. Just as Schubert was influenced by his teacher, Salieri, Weber inherited much from his teachers, Michael Haydn and Georg Vogler. The *E Flat Major Mass* (1818) is rich in harmonic and tonal effects. Solo and chorus sections, augmented to eight voices in the Sanctus, are underscored by an orchestral accompaniment rich in tonal value. Similarly, the *G Major* ("Jubilee") *Mass* (1819) is filled with expressive symbolism, making use of the leitmotiv. Because of external circumstances the solo received prominent treatment in Weber's church music.

The tendency toward symphonic church music was foreshadowed by the Mannheim school. The dramatic interpretation of the text, dictated by its mood and feeling, was replaced by the symphonic setting of the Viennese classical writers who gave church music a new importance in the realm of art, although they lost the feeling for its liturgical purpose.

Among the early contemporaries of Haydn and Mozart, Florian Gassmann (1729–1774), Johann Georg Reutter (1708–1772), Johann Ernst Eberlin (1702–1762), Anton Cajetan Adlgasser (1728–1777), Leopold Mozart (1719–1787), and others are characterized by greater contrapuntal depth.

MUSIC FOR CHURCH USE

The ordinary music for church use at the end of the eighteenth century and the beginning of the nineteenth was not produced by the Viennese classical composers.

In the fore among those who produced functional church music was Michael Haydn (1737–1806), Joseph Haydn's brother. He readily understood the importance of counterpoint and in his *Missae quadragesimales* he re-created the ancient polyphonic style. Graceful unpretentiousness in pleasing and unperplexed creativity is the characteristic of his art. This same spirit is evident in his German hymns. Everywhere he endeavored to escape the jaunty, entertainment type of church music and to create a style distinct from the secular media. Of special importance is his attraction to Gregorian chant. Like Johann Kaspar Ett later on, he enclosed the chant melody in simple harmonies, setting note against note.

Michael Haydn's work in church music is quite extensive. Besides the symphonic side of his work, he adopted, through his attitude toward chant and polyphony, many ideas of reform which had remarkable

Mass for Palm Sunday by M. Haydn, 1794

Chri - ste   e - lei - son

results in his own work but had little influence in his circle and did not lead to any general reform movement. His understanding of liturgical music was further demonstrated by the emphasis he placed on compositions for the Proper of the Mass.

In contrast to Michael Haydn's attitude of reform, most of the composers of the day endeavored to fit church-music work into the pattern of symphonic composition. These efforts are clearly seen in the numerous church compositions of Maximilian Stadler (1748–1833), Johann N. Hummel (1778–1837), and Joseph Eybler (1785–1846). On the other hand, a lighter church style, in imitation of Mozart, is found in the works, both grandiose and practical, of composers like Ditters von Dittersdorf (1739–1799), Leopold Hoffmann (1730–1793), Wenzel Pichl (1741–1805), John Baptist Wanhal (1739–1813), Ignaz Assmayer (1790–1862), Johann B. Gänsbacher (1778–1844), and many others. Franz Xaver Süssmayer's completion of Mozart's *Requiem* is indicative of his familiarity with his master's art. Unfortunately, his own ecclesiastical music, of a more practical kind, does not always show the same serious artistic creativeness, although it stands far above the mere trivial aping of Haydn's and Mozart's style seen in the so-called "country masses" of Anton Diabelli (1781–1858), Ambros Rieder (1771–1855), Simon Sechter (1788–1867), Joseph Preindl (1756–1823), Robert Führer (1807–1861), and countless others whose works enjoyed an extraordinary popularity even in the second half of the nineteenth century. Even if a truly artistic trait is to be detected here and there in these works, they are far removed from what was liturgically proper. Countless musicians continued, even in the second half of the nineteenth century, to further these efforts at creating a church music in German-speaking countries, but they only succeeded in producing works shallow both from the liturgical and artistic point of view.

The Bohemians, Johann Kozeluch (1738–1814), Johann Tomaschek

(1774–1850), Wenzel Horak (1800–1871), and others put their vital musical talents to work for the church without any regard at all for liturgical demands. Works intended for simple circumstances often were full of superficial mannerisms, e.g., in the compositions of Franz Gleissner (b. 1760), Johann Melchior Dreyer (c. 1735–1785), Franz Bühler (1760–1824), Karl Kempter (1819–1871), and many others who turned out hundreds of pieces for practical church use. All these compositions were directed to the musical taste of the crowd.

CHURCH MUSIC AND FOLK MUSIC

In the train of this bourgeois music, towns and villages also produced their own favorite art and created music not for the grand choirs of court or cathedral but for country choirs. Although the spread of musical culture resulted in a certain shallowness, church music did succeed in raising the general level of musical interest. Church choirs and orchestras were assembled from all segments of the population and fostered the study of music. Even in the simplest surroundings this often meant an astonishing development of musical life. The music for the Oberammergau Passion Play by Rocus Dedler is an example of this. Church music became music for entertainment, freed from its liturgical assignment, and in place of its ecclesiastical function it undertook the work of teaching music. As a result contemporary stylistic features were exaggerated, and stress was laid on the development of local peculiarities. Traits peculiar to Austria, Bavaria or the Rhineland left their mark on German church music, and this same feature was found in other countries as well. Lesser composers of Italy, France, Spain, and the Slavic countries, unencumbered by any "higher" artistic demands, put greater emphasis on local popular feeling than on the requirements of the liturgy. This was true with regard to music in Latin and in the vernacular. The distinction disappeared between liturgical and nonliturgical music, as well as between church music and secular compositions.

CHURCH MUSIC AT THE COURTS

Only the church music of the courts, true to the courtly taste, held to the Italian forms. The neo-Neapolitans, including Domenico Cimarosa

(1749–1801), Ferdinando Paer (1771–1839), and Pasquale Anfossi (1727–1797), performed their church music and their operas at court. Court composers, like Johann Gottlieb Naumann (1741–1801), Franz Seydelmann (1748–1806), and Joseph Schuster (1748–1812) worked at Dresden; Antonio Salieri (1750–1825), at Vienna; Peter von Winter (1754–1825) and Johann Kaspar Aiblinger (1779–1867), at Munich. The light *bel canto* style of the Neapolitans, based on the cantata, came to the fore, but especially in northern Italy there was a church music associated with the symphonic form. Its chief exponent was the German composer who worked in Bergamo, Simon Mayr (1763–1845).

CHURCH MUSIC IN THE ROMANCE COUNTRIES

Simon Mayr had great influence on church music in Italy. He strengthened the orchestra and the choral work as well. In spite of the emphasis on solo work, stress on choir and orchestra characterized the church music of Gaetano Donizetti (1797–1848) and Gioacchino Antonio Rossini (1792–1868). In Rossini's grandiose mass, sectional composition with a rich organ support is predominant. The Offertory, for orchestra, is a grand "Prélude religieux." The duet "Qui tollis," with solo harp accompaniment, shows the weakness of his style with its dramatic outbursts.

In his *Stabat Mater*, however, he achieved a more serious expression, especially in the great choruses with fugal ending. This new form of the Neapolitan cantata style was cultivated by Giuseppe Mercadante (1795–1870) and by most of the northern Italian masters of the first half of the nineteenth century.

In France, where the deterioration of church music had never moved in the direction of *bel canto*, the new efforts to develop choral and orchestral symphonic forms went on apace. At the beginning of the nineteenth century the Italian, Luigi Cherubini (1760–1842), the Swiss, Louis Niedermeyer (1802–1861), and the German, Sigismund Neukomm (1778–1858), a pupil of Haydn, together with Hector Berlioz (1803–1869), occupied the foreground in the symphonic church music of France. All of these wrote large concert works as well as smaller church compositions for practical use, significant for their closed symphonic form and their emphasis on declamation and musical phrase as expressive media in place of the Italian melodic devices. The solo ensemble, which is given the solo work in Haydn's masses, came to the fore in Cherubini's grand orchestral masses. Jean François Lesueur (1760–1837), Etienne Henri Méhul (1763–1817), and others followed this trend, with compositions in a picturesque and imitative style. In Hector Berlioz' great mass for the dead all media of dramatic force in his sonorous orchestral setting were made to serve ecclesiastical expression. In the *Dies irae* especially he displayed every effect of his art.

Even when liturgical forms were abandoned, the tendency in French music was to make the interpretation of the phrase more profound. It emphasized the text and its interpretation, in contrast to the general stressing of the music in Italian compositions of the period. This introduced a new attitude toward the text in which the great symphonic form was put aside in favor of a different manner of clothing the text, based on more ancient types. These efforts at reconstruction on historical models, combined with a renewed liturgical awareness, became the foundation for a reorientation of French church music in the later nineteenth century.

In Spain, too, similar tendencies were manifested in the eighteenth and nineteenth centuries. An old tradition of baroque *concertante* style did not permit church music in eighteenth-century Spain to grow shallow as it did in Italy. José de Torres y Martinez (1665–1738), J. F. de Tribarren (✝1760), and others continued to cultivate the ancient vocal polyphony and to make its influence felt even in the *stile moderno*. In the second half of the eighteenth century, the *concertante-cantata* forms were pushed aside by the symphonic form until the Romantic emphasis on mood evolved into the works of Rodriguez de Ledesma (1779–1848) and others.

In all these efforts to find greater artistic profundity, church music in the eighteenth century continued to be a stranger to its own liturgical task. In its purely musical development it lost a sense of its inner limitation by the liturgy and with this its other special and peculiar values.

CHURCH MUSIC IN AMERICA

The shallow symphonic church music of the eighteenth century and the early nineteenth was warmly welcomed in the Latin American countries where it found many imitators. The operatic style of church music with orchestral accompaniment, often nothing more than a secular composition with an ecclesiastical text, was very popular there.

This type of music likewise reached North America where an awakening interest in cultural achievements imported the style from Europe and introduced it into the church. Liturgical feeling was totally absent. A publication such as *The Morning and Evening Service of the Catholic Church*, edited by R. Garbett in 1840, containing Gregorian chants, was indeed a rarity. The inauguration at the start of the nineteenth century of choral and orchestral societies after the European fashion, especially the so-called "quartet choirs," was typical also of the artistic development of Catholic church music. An indication of the situation is given by John Walter when he notes that his *Ancient and Modern Music for the Use of the Catholic Church* (Baltimore, 1825) is "arranged for the pianoforte or organ." Superficial service music is also contained in the publications of J. B. David (1853, 1867), James Elliott (1855) and Anthony Werner (1857). For French-speaking congregations there appeared the *Recueil de Cantiques* (Baltimore, 1811) and for German congregations the *Katholische Gesang- und Gebetbuch* of B. H. F. Hellebusch (New York, 1858).

From the founding of Quebec French music of the baroque period, and later, was known and used in Canada. Subsequent English and Irish influences, brought in with the great immigrations of the nineteenth century, proved detrimental, since the English and Irish Catholics had no valid liturgical traditions. Hymnody in particular suffered.

Brazil was the only South American country with a spark of musical creativeness. J. M. N. Garcia (1767–1830), the most important of the older South American composers, wrote church music in imitation of Haydn.

Until the mid-1800s, therefore, Catholic church music in America had no valid, original life. Only later, when the reform movements in Germany and the liturgical movement in France began to have an effect also in the New World, did church music in America begin to take a more serious turn.

CHAPTER 15

Romantic Expression

MAKING CHURCH MUSIC MORE PROFOUND

In the nineteenth century a general reaction against the Enlightenment set in on all sides. In France, where the Revolution had annihilated all tradition, Chateaubriand (1768–1848) and De Maistre (1754–1821) laid the foundations for a new mode of thinking. In Germany, in the coterie of the Princess Gallitzin and in other like-minded circles, a new attitude toward the Church and in the Church slowly began to form. But the most important stir took place in the groups surrounding Johann M. Sailer (1751–1832) and Klemens M. Hofbauer (1751–1820). Everywhere there was a reappraisal of divine service and its outward display, and this naturally led to a radical change in church music.

Independent of the Caecilian reform movement (to be discussed later) which was in fact unknown to it, church music in the nineteenth century, after being alienated by the Enlightenment from its true foundation in art, sought on artistic grounds to regain forms that were liturgical in spirit and to return once more to its true role in Christian worship. It must be granted that this movement accomplished but little for services in country churches where the resources were scant. It did little likewise for vernacular hymnody. This gave some justification for the Caecilian Movement. In addition this artistic trend did nothing to promote the practical study and performance of the chant, in spite of the recognition and use of the Gregorian melodic treasury by so many composers represented in the movement, especially Franz Liszt.

Even in the later works of Schubert and Weber there is clear evidence that one characteristic of the Enlightenment, the obliteration of the line between secular and religious forms, had begun to disappear. The "art for art's sake" attitude was no longer prevalent. This development, based on artistic grounds, continued to grow till it reached a climax in Anton Bruckner, the last of the great proponents of symphonic church music.

CHURCH MUSIC IN FRANCE

In the works of Hector Berlioz and of his teacher, Jean François Lesueur (1763–1837), France at the beginning of the nineteenth century turned sharply toward a symphonic form that was more profound both ecclesiastically and artistically. The advance of a Catholic awareness in philosophy and theology in the first decades after the Revolution was evident in this art. As in the case of Simon Mayr, the increase of external resources meant an enlargement of the effect. These tendencies had great importance also in the works of Etienne Henri Méhul and Luigi Cherubini, and because of the regard they had for the smaller forms of practical church music, a technical refinement was manifested, especially in the church music of Charles Gounod (1818–1893). Classical clarity of form combined with a sickly sentimentality (e.g., *Ave Maria*, composed on the *C Major Prelude* of Bach) were the dominant traits of his work. The *Mass in Honor of St. Cecilia* (1882) was his greatest contribution to church music. Ancient classical polyphony was not without its influence in his compositions. In the same way, Charles Ambroise Thomas (1811–1896) and César Franck (1822–1890) made their contributions. In Franck's delicate harmonies — unfortunately, coupled with feeble melodies that at times are extremely sentimental — the composer gave the newer school of French music a significant stylistic medium. In his religious oratories and his organ music the magnificence of the symphonic form is still to be seen, but his vocal music was for the most part dedicated to the smaller practical types. Both the organ accompaniment to his few-voiced vocal works and his occasional use of solo instruments tended to accentuate the feebleness of his output. Along with Camille Saint-Saëns (1835–1921), Charles Bordes (1863–1909), Alexandre Guilmant (1837–1911), and Vincent d'Indy (1851–1931), César Franck promoted clarity of expression joined with delicate harmonic and tonal effectiveness. The core of this art was organ music and multivoiced extraliturgical religious music, for in France the chant movement dominated the field of liturgical music. As in the seventeenth and eighteenth centuries, the composition of liturgical organ music based on the chant continued together with the creation of the greater organ forms.

The efforts to establish a true art for the divine service which would be based on a contemporary stylistic foundation, and to set it side by side with the liturgical chant, were summed up in the founding of the Schola Cantorum. In 1894, twenty years after the establishment of the church-music school at Regensburg, the Schola Cantorum in Paris became the center of the French church-music movement. It differed from the Caecilian Movement in that it did not try to penetrate into every circumstance, which was the peculiar strength of Caecilianism. Neither did it undertake the reform of the church choir, nor put the reform of multivoiced church music in the foreground. In France there was little likelihood that the classical forms of practical church music, especially for the organ, would be elevated to expressive strength, or that the Caecilian type of practical music would become the vogue. Unlike Caecilian music, French composition retained its connection with the musical art as a whole, even though the feebleness of emotional expression of Jules Massenet, Camille Saint-Saëns, and others of that era turned to rank sentimentality in the shorter practical forms of church music. The French movement was interested not in creating anything completely new but in following the trends of evolution in the art as a whole, as well as developing the existing practice of church music. For this reason the French continued to preserve the chant that was found in the numerous editions of "plain chant," often revised and sentimentalized almost beyond recognition, despite the work being done at Solesmes. It was not until the publication of the Vatican edition that these publications gradually gave way. The Medicean version, in spite of the official character of the Regensburg edition, never gained any headway in France.

ARTISTIC EFFORTS IN GERMANY

In marked contrast to the French movement, in Germany the division was much greater between the reform movement (Caecilianism) and the continuing development and expansion of symphonic church music. Only Joseph Rheinberger (1839–1901) with his group in Munich, Johann Evangelista Habert (1833–1896), and the Austrian composers, maintained any connection with the progress of the musical art as a whole, or attempted to adapt it to less pretentious conditions as was done in France. Rheinberger's lyrical classicism produced lesser forms of practical music. Like the French, the greater part of his work was devoted to organ music. Besides the great *C Major Mass* with orchestra, there are his smaller masses and other church works with simple organ accompaniment. Outstanding sonorities, contrapuntal voice leading, suppleness in melody and harmony were the means he used for his rather romantic interpretation of the text. His forms and formal media were many-sided, and although in many of his motets and in his sonorous *E Flat Major Mass for Two Choruses* (1874) he sought a pure, vocal ideal, it was only in rare instances that his work attained any inner link with the liturgy. Rheinberger considered the *a cappella* ideal as the special medium for church. To it he subordinated even the organ accompaniment, although it appeared to be independent in its setting. Thus a new choral style was established, with its foundations in the secular and religious *a cappella* choruses of Franz Schubert, Robert Schumann and Johannes Brahms. In the same way, Peter Cornelius (1824–1874) wrote his *D Minor Mass* (1852), although he was also inspired by the historical contrapuntal style taught in Berlin. Similarly Louis Spohr (1784–1859) composed his seven-voiced mass on the same principles.

In contrast to this emphasis on the vocal line, Johannes Evangelista Habert attempted to achieve greater religious profundity with instrumental symphonic composition. In opposition to Franz Witt's Caecilian Society, he sought to establish a church-music movement in Austria. Moritz Brosig (1815–1887) in Breslau, and the Silesian coterie that surrounded him and Joseph Ignaz Schnabel (1767–1831), also sought to give depth to church music along the same lines. The symphonic form was also the starting point for the church music of Anton Dvořak (1841–1904) and the Bohemian masters, but with a stronger emphasis on vocalism. The extreme attitude toward vocal music that characterized Caecilianism was important within the movement and also for its influence on its opponents. Romanticism, too, discovered the vocal ideal for religious music, and even subordinated instrumental accompaniment to it. Even in the opera, religious scenes were characterized by the use of *a cappella* vocal music.

Franz Liszt (1811–1866) was completely captivated by this effort. The grand tonal art of the Romantic school conditioned his instrumentally accompanied church music. In the *Gran Mass* (1855) and the *Hungar-*

ian Coronation Mass (1867) there are delicate delineations of mood ranging from tender tonal pleasure to effects of strength and power. In the manner of the dramatic art of his programmatic symphonies, Liszt tried to extract from the text every possible musical effect. There is a remarkable contrast in his *Mass for Male Choir* (1848), his *Requiem* (1868) and especially in his *Missa choralis* (1862). In these he interprets the words along the lines of the older polyphonic art. Although liturgical expression often appears to be supplanted by the inventions of his own personal emotion, Liszt created out of the contemporary thought and artistic form a music for worship that would come to life only in the liturgy itself. However, the fundamental attitude of his art was determined by the drama and individuality of writing. This is most clearly seen in his program music which is the manifestation of his particular artistic genius.

Liszt differs fundamentally from Anton Bruckner (1824–1896), whose symphonic work was not an individual portrayal in terms of an extra-musical program, but a natural and simple music used as the vehicle of common experience. Bruckner's basic attitude was much closer to the universal and the objective than was Liszt's. He approached the liturgical text with the profound comprehension of his art, so characteristic of the German composer, and with the reverence of a deeply religious man. In his work the text breaks forth into awesome worship. The mighty, jubilant *Te Deums* (1881, 1884), and the *Ecce sacerdos* (1885) stand side by side with the devout prayerfulness of his three great masses, in *D Minor* (1864), *F Minor* (1866), and *E Minor* (1868). Palestrina contrived to make the polyphony of the motet setting a perfect expression of liturgical prayer, and Bruckner achieved the breadth of the symphonic structure by using sonorities determined by the composition. For Palestrina text and setting became a unit, and for Bruckner the profundity of prayer made the text a powerful theme in its symphonic realization. In spite of the manifold development of harmony and tonality, choral construction is preserved in the latter's writings. The borrowed chant theme is indeed shaped anew, but in the total plan the attitude of prayer is retained. Bruckner created a liturgical mode of expression built on the symphonic development of the nineteenth century. The true ecclesiastical style that Witt and the Caecilians were striving for, utilizing the resources of the contemporary symphonic technique, was found in ideal form in the work of Bruckner. However, the Caecilians, failing to recognize it for what it was, overlooked it and disregarded it. The orchestra was important in

Bruckner's church music, but the accent was still on the vocal line. The orchestra depended on the voices in contrast to the Viennese classicists, who assimilated the voices into the instrumental lines. The use of wind instruments in the orchestral setting brought out the vocal line clearly. In his *E Minor Mass*, Bruckner employed no strings and simply united a wind orchestra to the vocal composition. By the profundity of its concept his work succeeded in gaining a close union with the liturgy. Although some of his lesser compositions were not great, others, like the motet *Os justi* (1879), using the simplest means, became models of the most profound ecclesiastical expression. The preference for *a cappella* work in Bruckner's smaller church compositions shows the same recognition of values as his larger works. Bruckner's compositions represent the highest development of a truly ecclesiastical symphonic art, just as the works of Palestrina manifest the climax of sixteenth-century polyphony as liturgical music. In the sixteenth century it was an Italian who created the most ideal artistic form for liturgical prayer; in the nineteenth, it was an Austrian, Bruckner, who shaped the great instrumental development of his people into an ideal liturgical expression.

CHURCH MUSIC IN ITALY

The dramatic art, which began in the seventeenth century, became the means for achieving greater depth in church music during the nineteenth century in Italy. Conductors were expected to compose works for the great solemnities either as part of their regular assignment or on special commission. Eighteenth-century customs of cathedral and court choirs were preserved into the nineteenth century. Most composers of opera also wrote for the church on commission, but they treated the liturgical text much as they did a libretto, making it the opportunity for dramatic effect or lyric expression of mood. Following Simon Mayr, the greatest exponent of this type of grand composition was Giuseppe Verdi (1813–1901). His writing was not liturgical art either by intention or by its intrinsic construction. In fact, because of its subjective, dramatic quality it could never be considered liturgical expression.

Like Caecilianism in Germany, the reform movement in Italy stood apart from the general musical evolution. The efforts of Guerrino Amelli (1848–1933), and Angelo de Santi (1847–1922) were directed in the main to the cultivation of Gregorian chant. Ecclesiastical decrees gave the movement momentum, while the work of the German Caecilian Society influenced Italian efforts for reform.

CHURCH MUSIC IN BELGIUM

In Belgium, where the Institute of Mechlin was founded in 1879 by Nicholas Jacques Lemmens (1823–1881), the reform movement was put into closer touch with the whole musical development by Edgar Tinel (1854–1911). Caecilianism in Germany regarded the polyphony of Palestrina as the ideal of multivoiced Catholic music, but Tinel saw in Johann Sebastian Bach the great art of Christian expression that should be the foundation of Catholic church music. The French organ school that surrounded César Franck and Alexandre Guilmant had already revived Bach's art and made it the basis of its own efforts. As a pupil of Adolph Hesse (1809–1863) in Breslau, Lemmens found himself at the very center of the German Bach cult. In Tinel's work counterpoint in the style of Bach is the basis of composition. What urged him to view Bach's work as the starting point for a new development in church music was the spiritual attitude of this art, its living faith and devotion which extended beyond denominational limits and suggested a new principle in opposition to stiff formalism. This was a novel attempt at solving the artistic problem of church music. Although it was much discussed theoretically, it actually achieved very little.

CHAPTER 16

Efforts at Reform

HISTORICAL FORMS OF CHURCH MUSIC

The change in thinking and in attitude toward religion at the beginning of the nineteenth century occasioned a reorientation of theology, the ecclesiastical arts and forms of prayer. What contemporary church music and ecclesiastical thought could not offer these new efforts was sought for in history. Accordingly, while contemporary currents were rejected, historical forms were accepted. But this strict trend in church music segregated itself from the general musical development. The ecclesiastical graphic arts found a classic mold in the ideals of what was known as the Nazarene school of painting. Similarly, Anton Friedrich Thibaut (1825) rediscovered in ancient classic polyphony the neo-humanist clarity of declamation and a universal ideal of composition that provided the "purity of tonal art" that the reformers were seeking. This line of thought led back to the liturgical song of the Middle Ages, making Gregorian chant and ancient classical polyphony the two supporting pillars of church music in the nineteenth century. This gave a new impetus to the cultivation of the *stile antico*.

A CAPPELLA STYLES IN ROMANCE COUNTRIES

In Italy and France the transition was slow, while in Germany the re-evaluation of polyphony was much more basic. Giuseppe Jannaconi

(1741–1816), Stanislas Mattei (1750–1825), Nicolo Zingarelli (1752–1837), Fortunato Santini, Giuseppe Baini, Pietro Alfieri and many lesser composers strove to unite the techniques of ancient polyphony and contemporary expression.

Alfieri, op. 62 (1852)

A - - - ni - ma Chri - sti sanc - ti - fi - ca me

Because of this conscious departure from the current musical language the composition was frequently stiff and devoid of all artistic expression.

However, in their work as a whole, and in their research, Giuseppe Baini (1775–1844), Fortunato Santini (1778–1862), and Pietro Alfieri (1801–1863) did revive ancient polyphony in its original form. Their performances and especially their large collections of ancient scores had an important influence on church-music practice. Originating in the tra-

Ave Maria for Three Male Voices by G. Baini

Al - le - lu - ja, al - le - lu - ja, al - le - lu -

dition of the *stile antico*, the revival of ancient classical polyphony in Italy became the focal point for a restoration of polyphony in all countries. Alexandre Choron (1772–1834) and Juste Adrien de Lafage (1801–1862) were in this tradition, as were the Germans Johann Kaspar Aiblinger (1779–1867), Karl Proske (1794–1861), Theodor Witt (1823–1855), who started an edition of the collected works of Palestrina, Raphael Kiesewetter (1773–1850), Karl von Winterfeld (1784–1852), Georg Poelchau (1773–1836), Otto Nicolai (1810–1848), Ernst Theodor Amadeus Hoffmann (1766–1850), and others. In 1811, Alexandre Choron was charged with the reform of church music in France. The strict Italian polyphony of the sixteenth century was his ideal, as is shown in his *Principes de composition* (3 vols., 1808) and in his *Encyclopédie musicale* (8 vols., 1836–1838). His writings, his organizational work (*Maîtrise*), and his music school (Ecole royale de chant) led the way toward a deepening and strengthening of church music. This path was followed and broadened by Abraham Louis Niedermeyer (1802–1861) who reopened Choron's school under the name Ecole Niedermeyer. Pierre Dietsch (1808–1865) and others also contributed to the reform in France on the basis of historical forms.

Thus, alongside the symphonic, dramatic church music of the nineteenth century, there grew up a new style, based on history and committed to fulfilling liturgical demands. While in returning to ancient models it broke with contemporary symphonic techniques, it tried at the same time to adjust and influence contemporary music. The basis for these efforts was the liturgical awakening that followed the work of Dom Prosper Guéranger in the mid-nineteenth century. On this foundation the medieval liturgical melodies were reassessed. In France, in fact, chief interest soon settled on the medieval liturgical chant, overshadowing the revival of *a cappella* polyphony. In Spain, Pérez y Gascón, Miguel Hilarion Eslava (1807–1878) and others fostered a vocal style based on older principles.

CHURCH MUSIC REFORM IN GERMANY

In Germany, at the beginning of the nineteenth century, two important centers of reform were begun at Munich and at Regensburg. By his performance of Allegri's *Miserere* in 1816, Johann Kaspar Ett (1788–1847) took the first step in the revival of the old Italian art. In his earlier music Ett still paid homage to the traditional principles of composition, but in his later years the *a cappella* setting became his usual composition. His great masses (1821, 1829, 1846), his *Miserere* (1823) and other works were masterpieces in the new trend. Gregorian melodies dominated many of his *a cappella* compositions, and this use of the chant brought him close to the liturgy. In the manner of Michael Haydn he frequently used a chant melody as the upper voice in an *a cappella* setting.

Johann Kaspar Aiblinger (1779–1867), like Ett, followed the reform style. The tenderness of expression in his Marian compositions and the instrumental masses and motets is easily felt even in his use of the old strict style, particularly because he combines harmonic devices with the contrapuntal technique.

An a cappella Mass by Aiblinger (Agnus Dei)

The reform movement had an influence also on Joseph Hartmann Stuntz, Franz Lachner and other leading musicians in Munich during the first half of the nineteenth century. J. B. Schmid and Johann Michael Hauber were concerned with the pastoral importance of the movement, while Johann Michael Sailer and Martin Deutinger gave it a sound theological foundation; and Karl Greith, Karl Drobisch, and Eduard Rottmanner contributed to its progress also. Nevertheless the movement had little impact, especially because the more recent principles of composition were too freely mixed with the traditional forms. Gottlieb Tucher (1798–1877) and Karl Schafhäutl (1803–1890) caused some stir with their scientific and historical studies.

A greater success was achieved by the reforms that emanated from Regensburg about the same time. Karl Proske (1794–1861) was the chief figure. In Italy he collected old manuscripts and editions to make a selection available in his *Musica divina*. He presented practical performances of the ancient works and by his public efforts he endeavored to interest civil and ecclesiastical authorities in the need for church-music reform. He found eager promoters of his ideas in his own bishop, Johann

Michael Sailer, and in the enthusiastic patron of art, King Ludwig I. Thus the reform spread all over the country.

Everywhere an appreciation of ancient church music awakened, and a sense of its particular value apart from the trends of music in general was felt. Romanticism carried these ideas into Protestant church music, resulting in the introduction of Italian church music and the rediscovery of the wealth of the German chorale and German church music of the sixteenth century. Richard Wagner supported the movement in his writing and activities. In all the great ecclesiastical centers the reform made progress. Church music was freed from secularized influences and a new art, fitted to the demands of the liturgy, grew up on the foundations of the earlier style. Among those who fostered the reform were Simon Sechter in Vienna; Michael Töpler, A. G. Stein and Friederich Heimsoeth in Cologne; Stephen Lück, Heinrich Oberhoffer and Michael Hermesdorf in Trier; Bernhard Quante in Münster; and Benz in Speyer.

Of course, the country at large was scarcely touched by this Romantic trend or by the new currents in church music. The accomplishment of this task was reserved to Franz Witt and his Caecilian Society.

REVIVAL OF GREGORIAN CHANT

Proceeding apace with the revival of ancient classic polyphony and the creation of new works based on it, interest in Gregorian chant increased under the influence of Romanticism. The recognition of worship as "the artistic work of the community," coupled with study on the history of the liturgy, led to the original liturgical music. Of course, Gregorian chant had been retained all through the centuries, but its meaning within the framework of the liturgy had been lost and in many places it was set aside at the service in favor of symphonic compositions. The liturgical awareness of the Romanticists restored it to its rightful place in worship. Johann Kaspar Ett sought to accomplish this by further simplification of the melodic line which had already been much abbreviated in the reform versions of the eighteenth century. He desired simplicity and clarity. In his *Cantica sacra* (1827) he published a version that was predominantly syllabic with a thorough-bass accompaniment that emphasized harmonic accents that were forced on the chant. Although this work of Ett's did little justice to the reality of the medieval liturgical melody, it did arouse interest in the chant, so that it was no longer regarded as a mere substitute for multivoiced singing. At first this newly awakened interest was confined to the shortened versions of the eighteenth century, each different from the other, but by the middle of the century there was a growing effort to reconstruct the original version. The chant studies of Johann Baptist Schiedermayer (1828), Joseph Antony (1829), and Maslon (1839) were based on local reformed versions. This was true also in Italy and France, as the works of Pietro Alfieri (1835) and Theodore Nisard (1846) show, while in Spain, an older chant tradition was preserved. The revival of the historical study of music included the search for a more ancient and universal chant version. Study of this problem was advanced by the discovery of Codex 359 of St. Gall by Ildefons von Arx and by the writings of Anselm Schubiger, Louïs Lambillotte, Theodore Nisard, Jean Louis Danjou, François Fétis and others. In 1848, Edmond Duval and de Voght published a volume of chant, called the Mechlin edition, which was based on the Medicean version of 1614. The *Graduale* of Rheims and Cambrai, 1851, was the first edition of the traditional medieval chant based on the Codex Montpellier, discovered in 1847. This research stemmed from the liturgical work of the abbot of Solesmes, Prosper Guéranger, and the Catholic restoration movement inaugurated in France in the third decade of the nineteenth century. At the command of Dom Guéranger, two monks of Solesmes, Dom Paul Jausion, and later Dom Joseph Pothier, undertook to reconstruct the ancient version; their work appeared in the Solesmes publications, which were the basis for the Vatican edition.

In Germany, similar studies were undertaken by Karl Schafhäutl, Raimund Schlecht, Michael Hermesdorf, Peter Bohn and others. They also turned their attention to local German versions which they partly revived. At Beuron a center for both practical and theoretical study of chant was established. In Switzerland the Gregorian movement was given its strongest impulse by Anselm Schubiger.

The Gregorian problem became essentially a historical one. By the middle of the nineteenth century numerous editions of the melodies were readied, making the results of these various researches available for practical use. The multiplicity of the versions, however, and the quarrel over their historical accuracy soon alienated the whole movement from its original liturgical starting-point. Franz X. Haberl prepared a version based on the Medicean edition. This was authorized by the Sacred Congregation of Rites, and the firm of Pustet in Regensburg published the *Graduale* (1871, 1873) and the *Antiphonale* (1878). They received little more than passing recognition, although the effort put a sudden block in the way of further advance in the restoration of the chant. The great upsurge of liturgical feeling connected with the Romanticism of the first half of the nineteenth century was suddenly paralyzed in the middle of the century. It appeared that only organized measures could promote the reform of church music and renew it generally.

THE CAECILIAN EFFORTS

Franz Xaver Witt (1834–1888), through his Caecilian Society, created the organization which brought church-music reform especially to countries using the German language. These groups sprang up in great numbers among people of every intellectual and financial status. Because of their number and their decisive purpose they exercised a great influence. The novelty of the ideas propounded caused the real importance of other reform efforts already undertaken elsewhere to be unjustly overlooked. In some places there was opposition to the dictatorial tone of Witt's organization. In 1868, Witt founded the Caecilian Society at Bamberg, and in 1870 he obtained papal approbation. He publicized his reform ideas in two church-music periodicals, *Fliegende Blätter für katholischen Kirchenmusik* (1886) and *Musica sacra* (1868), but by 1865 he had already started the war against the shallow church music of his age by publishing a booklet on "The Condition of Church Music in Old Bavaria." The writings of Stephen Lück (1856), Joseph Proksch (1858), Raimund Schlecht (1861), G. Stein (1864) and others had anticipated and prepared for the struggle. Bernhard Quante (1867), Anselm Schubiger (1869) and Karl Böhm (1875) proposed similar reform ideas, and Heinrich Oberhoffer (1862) and Johannes Evangelista Habert (1868) supplemented the movement in various periodicals.

In France, Joseph d'Ortigue (1854), Couturier (1862), Ludovic Celler (1867) and others emphasized the requirements for a general reform of church music and publicized these notions in the magazine *Maîtrise* (1857). In Italy, the fight was taken up by V. Meini (1863) and others. Church synods beginning with the third decade of the nineteenth century were concerned with liturgical questions and musical problems and this led to various episcopal ordinances. In 1868, the Schola Gregoriana was established at the Lateran by Pope Pius IX. Everywhere interest in church music developed. Organizations patterned on the German Caecilian Society were erected and spread the ideas of reform in Holland (1868), North America (1873), Bohemia (1874), Upper Austria (1875), Ireland (1876), Belgium (1880), Poland and Hungary (1897). Associated with Witt in the German Caecilian Society was Franz Xaver Haberl (1840–1910), whose work as a music historian and theorist is known through his *Magister choralis* (1875) and his edition of the collected works of Palestrina (1881) and other musicological research. Another associate was the composer Michael Haller (1840–1915), who was successful in imitating the old *a cappella* style. In the Rhineland, Franz Nekes (1844–1914) wrote in the strict polyphonic style.

AIM AND ACCOMPLISHMENT OF THE CAECILIANS

Although the ancient *a cappella* style was the ideal of the Caecilian movement, Witt also desired to promote the new church music with organ or orchestral accompaniment and to include it within his reforms. Chant, ancient polyphony, new *a cappella* music and new instrumentally accompanied works were all part of the area of reform, along with the vernacular hymn. Witt's reform was to embrace not only cathedrals but village churches. He had to provide suitable materials for all. He himself wrote works for all circumstances. Hundreds of persons, often with more good will than ability, contributed compositions from which publishers expected to make great financial success. Thus, along with many valuable works, a flood of poor Caecilian church music was printed. It was accepted indiscriminately and even judged to be good as long as the text was complete and the composition was diatonic and simple. At times even the name of a writer, from whom one could expect a liturgical aim, was taken as a criterion, even though all artistic meaning was absent from the composition. Music was apparently often prepared from a few cadences and stereotyped phrases, with the knowledge that it could be widely disseminated by recommendation of the organization in the "Catalog of the Society of St. Caecilia." This list served to outlaw such purely dance-like church music as that of Johann Baptist Schiedermayer, Wenzel Hôrack and Franz Schöpf, only to replace it with pedestrian compositions without artistic worth. Many valuable works created outside the Caecilian circle were overlooked, and some of the better material produced by the Caecilians themselves was eclipsed. Mere externalism resulted and alienated church music from true liturgical and artistic experience. This could only bring the whole movement into disrepute. The shallowness that was supposed to be overcome in other spheres returned to church music by a different route, and prevented it from attaining that liturgical depth for which such earnest preparations were undertaken in the second quarter of the nineteenth century.

Although most compositions did not fulfill their artistic role, some groundwork was laid. The ideal of the polyphonic *a cappella* style gained importance as a teaching device even beyond the realm of church music. The strict contrapuntal teaching of Johann Joseph Fux was not forgotten. Johann Gottfried Bellermann's *Kontrapunkt* (1862) was the basic theoretical work for the late nineteenth century. Through the work of Michael Haller (*Kontrapunkt*, 1891), Franz Nekes, Gerhard Quadflieg, Peter Piel, August Wiltberger and others, composition in the strict style became the common method for teaching church music. The works of these men lacked inventiveness as did those of John Singenberger, Friedrich Koenen (1829–1887), J. N. Ahle, J. Auer and others. Nevertheless, they put the technique of composing on a solid footing. The early works of Peter Griesbacher and the *a cappella* polyphonic compositions of Michael Haller and Franz Nekes were certainly of value. The many endeavors, too, to combine strict composition with newer forms of expression, such as the efforts of Karl Greith, Gustav Edward Stehle (1839–1915), Ignatz Mitterer, and Ludwig Bonvin, could be justified, even though there was always the danger of stylistic conflict. Nevertheless, the effort to create an appropriate music in the spirit of the liturgy led to a sharp separation of the church style from the general development of music. This contrasted with the efforts of others who sought to eliminate the boundaries by means of a symphonic church style. Earlier efforts attempted to make a contribution to religious expression with art as a starting point; Caecilianism endeavored to create a musical form from an ecclesiastical vantage point. This was the revolutionary attitude of the Caecilian Movement, and it held a danger of negating the artistic. Moreover, in the attempt to obtain a doctrinaire objectivity in expression, a wealth of national peculiarities that distinguished other church-music currents was unfortunately lost.

THE CAECILIAN MOVEMENT OUTSIDE GERMANY

Although the movement begun by Franz Witt in Germany was most successful in German-speaking lands, it was not confined to them. The reform was also effective, to some extent, in Italy, especially as the result of the founding by Witt of the *Scuola Gregoriana* in Rome in 1880, and the formation of the Society of St. Caecilia through the efforts of Angelo de Santi, who became the first director of the Pontifical School of Sacred Music in 1911. In addition, there were the parallel movements centering on the efforts of Giuseppe Baini, Fortunato Santini, and Pietro Alfieri. In Czechoslovakia, a Society of St. Cyril was established in 1873, and there, as well as in Jugoslavia, a Caecilian Society was formed in 1877. Ireland felt the movement especially through the efforts of Henry Bewerunge, a pupil of Franz Xaver Haberl at Regensburg, who began to teach at St. Patrick's, Maynooth, in 1888. Hungary followed in 1897, as well as Holland and Belgium. A similar society was also founded in Spain, but not until 1912.

By far the greatest success outside Germany was won in the United States, mainly through the efforts of John B. Singenberger (1848–1924). Archbishop John Martin Henni, who had started an American Caecilian Society in Cincinnati in 1838, founded the Catholic Normal School of the Holy Family in Milwaukee in 1871. To this foundation came Singenberger and Max Spiegler, both imbued with the spirit of the German reform movement. A few months after his arrival, in 1873, Singenberger, with the help of Joseph Salzmann, then rector of Holy Family Normal School, formally instituted the American Caecilian Society. Even in its first years it counted three thousand members. The music of the German Caecilians was performed, German publications were used, and both plain song and polyphony were studied. The official publication of the society, *Caecilia*, a monthly, was first printed in 1874, at first in German, later in English. John Singenberger, his son Otto Singenberger, Dom Ermin Vitry and Theodore Marier were among the editors of this magazine. In 1957, this periodical was transferred to a new organization called the Society of St. Caecilia, and it is now published as a quarterly under the aegis of this group, with Msgr. Francis Schmitt as editor.

Two major publishing firms specializing in church music were founded about this time: in 1864, that of J. Fischer and Bros., in Dayton, Ohio; and in 1895, the M. L. Nemmers Co. of Milwaukee. The German firm of Pustet of Regensburg established two branch offices, one in New York in 1865, and another in Cincinnati in 1867.

As a composer John Singenberger showed a marvelous talent, although his work is uneven. He followed the Caecilian principles strictly, as did

Hubert Gruender (1870–1940), Henry Tappert, Joseph J. Pierron (b. 1875), Martin G. Dumler, Melchiore Mauro-Cottone, and others.

THE GREGORIAN CHANT

The chant and the vernacular hymn had their special place in these reform attempts. Because of the emphasis on liturgical requirements, song in the vernacular was banned from the liturgical service, although this did not actually occur everywhere. The study and practice of chant was based on the Regensburg edition, which took over the revised Medicean version without critical insight into its shortcomings. Little consideration was given to the question of genuine artistry in multivoiced composition or in chant. The interpretation of the melodic line and the harmonic accompaniment followed contemporary modes of thought. Harmonic accompaniment was taken for granted, and was shaped in accordance with the harmonic principles of ancient classical polyphony. The aimless harmonies found in Mettenleiter's *Enchiridion chorale* (1853) were typical of the numerous chant accompaniments prepared by the Caecilians. Although the purity of the diatonic line was safeguarded, little account was taken of the essence of the chant or the accents of the melodic line. The ancient music was more encumbered by the superposed and stereotyped harmonic accents than it was by the errors in the Medicean melodies themselves. Besides adding an accompaniment, the Caecilians further attempted to promote a harmonic evaluation of the chant by means of faux-bourdon settings resembling their multivoiced compositions. Countless editions from the sixteenth century, in addition to many new compositions in this manner, made it possible to avoid singing Vespers in the Gregorian chant alone.

THE VERNACULAR HYMN

One weighty problem faced by the German Caecilian reform was that of the vernacular hymn. The reform undertook a double task: to relegate the vernacular hymn to extraliturgical services; and to free it from the secularized attitude of the Enlightenment. The latter was accomplished by a return to the ancient treasury of hymnody as well as by new composi-

tions. At the beginning of the nineteenth century efforts were made to
delve more deeply into the history of the hymn. These efforts revived
many Latin hymns based on chant as well as hymns of the sixteenth and
seventeenth centuries. Jäck (1817), Weinzierl (1817), Knievel (1840),
Pressar (1844), and Dreves (1846) worked on the early Latin hymns.
Toepler (1832), Schmidt (1836), Schnepper (1841), Lück (1846), and
Bone (1847) contributed their efforts toward Renaissance and Baroque
hymns. And some diocesan hymnals, among them Cologne (1830),
Speyer (1842), and Augsburg (1859) utilized these older hymns which
the Romanticists' historicism favored. Many of these were also included
in collections made by Bone (1847), Stein (1853), Mohr (1862, 1881,
1891), Tilike (1864), Baur (1868), and others. Thus a great store of
the older hymns became part of countless Caecilian hymnals, although

L. Lambillotte, Cantiques 1859

many Baroque and rationalistic hymns were retained also. Contemporary composers contributed very few worthwhile hymns to the treasury of popular ecclesiastical song. Johann Kaspar Aiblinger (1845) and Anselm Schubiger (1845) composed hymns in a folk-song style, and these were imitated by Michael Haller, Mitterer, and others. Besides the congregational hymn we also find German devotional hymns for several voices, but their dry and unemotional artificiality, or their spurious sentimentality, for the most part was inappropriate both for ecclesiastical or popular expression.

Other countries, too, produced a large literature of such *cantiques, inni,* etc., but in most cases there was an absence both of authenticity of experience and artistic craftsmanship. Artificial folk songs could ill correspond to true popular devotion. In France, the hymns of Louis Lambillotte became very popular. The piano style of the accompaniment was as much a part of these hymns as it was of the Marian hymns of Johann Kaspar Aiblinger, which they surpassed in shallowness of melodic expression.

Although these creations in the vernacular seldom measured up to their role as extraliturgical song, they did arouse interest and through the revival of older hymns they helped lay a foundation for a new development. The greatest results of this movement were found in Holland where the Flemish hymn was successfully imitated.

SEARCH FOR A CONTEMPORARY CHURCH STYLE

By the end of the nineteenth century the Caecilian Movement began to lose the strength of its first impact. In many of its trends it hardened into mere formalism; it became an organization in place of a movement. Little creative power followed the return to ancient polyphony, and the revival and reappraisal of the old sixteenth-century works, as well as the liturgical melodies, were unable to lay the foundation either for more intelligent worship or more vital artistry. In the graphic arts, the triumph over the inflexible Nazarene school and the external copying of Romanesque and Gothic forms resulted in the end of a stiff sacred style. So in music Caecilianism was bound to be shaken in the pursuit of its own rigid purpose. It was necessary to recognize other trends that had been hitherto ignored, because contemporary artistic forms of expression had to be considered as possibilities in the formation of an ecclesiastical art.

Peter Griesbacher (1864–1933), whose early *a cappella* works, along with those of Haller and Nekes, were among the best imitations of the ancient style, soon changed to a contemporary idiom. Chromaticism and the use of leitmotiv, which were among the most important media used by Richard Wagner a half century previously, suddenly became of value and interest in church-music composition. In the same doctrinaire and formal manner that the older Caecilians employed in establishing diatonic polyphony as the basis for an ecclesiastical style, Griesbacher now lauded chromaticism and the use of leitmotiv. But what he brought to the fore were only external stylistic media which, robbed of their foundation in the structure of the work as a whole, became meaningless and soon degenerated into mere superficiality. In spite of his theoretical writings, Griesbacher unwittingly became the promoter of shallowness in church music. Like Wagner's decadent successors, Griesbacher lacked an intrinsic need for using these media of expression, and this led to a distortion and counterfeiting of style.

Although Griesbacher's attempt to utilize the contemporary idiom led to an inartistic sentimentality and consequently did nothing to solve the question of Caecilian rigidity, it was of prime importance for church music. By his complete, dogmatic break with the Caecilian concept, the restricting of a sacred style to mere externals was upset and new life was breathed into church music. More liberal trends within Caecilianism itself were recognized, as well as other efforts striving for a church-music ideal.

Rheinberger's pupil, Joseph Renner, still had to defend his own artistic development against narrow Caecilian criticisms in his work on *Modern Church Music and Chant* (1902), but gradually there arose a sympathetic appreciation of an ecclesiastical art free in the choice of the expressive media it employed. As a result Joseph Rheinberger and his school obtained a fairer appraisal. At the beginning of the twentieth century recognition was given to the Viennese composers, August Weirich (1858–1921) Josef Vockner (1842–1906) and Josef Venantius von Wöss (1863–1943), who was influenced by Anton Bruckner. The Silesian school developed around Moritz Brosig, and included the renowned Max Filke (1855–1911). Other composers of the period were the Alsatians, Franz Xaver Mathias (1871–1939) and Joseph Maria Erb (1858–1944), Joseph Pembauer (1848–1923), Adalbert Rihovsky (b. 1871) and many others who sought their own artistic ecclesiastical expression. In the Caecilian camp, along with Peter Griesbacher, the chief proponents and supporters of a contemporary church style were Vincenz Goller (b. 1873) and Max

Springer (b. 1877). So, at the beginning of the twentieth century church music found itself in a situation much changed in regard to the older attitude of Caecilianism, and also in regard to those numerous earnest currents outside the Caecilian Movement. What was true of Germany was true also of other countries where, by and large, the narrow restrictions of the Caecilian Movement had not found a place. Nearly everywhere there was a revival of church-music endeavor. In Italy new paths were made by Lorenzo Perosi (1872–1956) and Enrico Bossi (1861–1925); they were followed by Salvatore Gallotti (1856–1928), Ernesto Boezi (1856–1946), Giovanni Telbaldini (1864–1952), Oreste Ravanello (1871–1938), Raffaele Casimiri (1880–1943) and Licinio Refice (1885–1954). In France the lead in this new trend was taken by the Schola Cantorum group.

MOTU PROPRIO OF 1903

Whenever church music breaks new ground, church authorities must take a stand. This happened at the beginning of the twentieth century in a more systematic and comprehensive form than ever before in papal pronouncements. The motu proprio of Pius X, dated November 22, 1903, became the basic document of church-music legislation, evaluating the issues and antitheses of the nineteenth century and stressing the principle of artistic freedom in relation to the liturgy.

According to the motu proprio the traditional Gregorian chant, used by priest, choir and people, occupies the first place in church music. It possesses, in the highest degree, the qualities proper to the liturgy, "sanctity, goodness of form and universality," without, however, challenging the characteristics peculiar to each country and race. In the second place stands ancient classical polyphony, especially that of the Roman school of Palestrina. In the third place is modern music, with its many stylistic forms, insofar as they are appropriate to the liturgical texts, and insofar as they avoid all that is theatrical and unseemly. The importance of the text and the vocal character of church music demand a curtailment of instrumental accompaniment, although recognition is given to the organ. In addition to directives about the music itself, regulations were given governing the performers because of their close connection with the liturgy. Means for carrying out the instructions and suggestions for the musical training of the clergy and singers conclude the motu proprio.

Other papal pronouncements followed. The *Regolamento* for church music in Rome (1912) brought clarifications and supplementary regulations. The *Codex juris canonici* (1917) contained only general requirements. In the apostolic constitution of Pius XI, *Divini cultus sanctitatem* (1928), certain particulars were re-emphasized, especially the musical training of the clergy, the liturgical choir (boys' choir), congregational chant, and organ playing. Thus twice in twenty-five years the popes issued authoritative pronouncements regarding church music. Earlier decisions, like the *Regolamento* for church music in Italy (1884), were concerned primarily with the prohibition of secular trends, but Pius X and Pius XI issued positive commands for vital cultivation of liturgical music.

TRADITIONAL GREGORIAN CHANT

The Caecilian Society assisted in obtaining, in the Regensburg edition of the chant, official recognition for the Medicean version of 1614, at the very time when earnest studies were being made everywhere to re-establish the traditional medieval chant. Especially in France, in connection with the liturgical renewal, a revival of the genuine melodies was actually making progress. In 1880, Dom Joseph Pothier established the theoretical principles of the ancient art. In 1883, he published the *Liber gradualis* and in 1895, the *Liber antiphonarius* and the *Liber responsorialis*. In Germany, the circle of Raimund Schlecht, Michael Hermesdorf and the Choralverein fought for an old German version of the chant. In 1882, a Gregorian congress held at Arezzo insisted on the spuriousness of the Regensburg version and asked for a revival of the traditional liturgical melodies. One of the participants at this congress was Giuseppe Sarto, later Pius X. In spite of opposition from the editor of the Regensburg edition, Franz Xaver Haberl, Pustet (the publisher) and even the Congregation of Rites, these Gregorian studies continued. Finally in 1901, at the termination of Pustet's thirty-year printing privilege, Pope Leo XIII acknowledged these new labors, especially of the Benedictines of Solesmes, and thus introduced the chant reform.

In the motu proprio of 1903 it was decided to publish the *Editio Vaticana* on the basis of the genuine chant tradition as guaranteed by historical studies. But even as late as 1902, after the appearance of Raphael Molitor's basic investigation of the post-Tridentine reform (1901), Franz Xaver Haberl still attempted to defend the Regensburg edition in his *Geschichte und Wert der offiziellen Choralbücher*. Scholars, musicians and the Church itself demanded historical authenticity for the liturgical melodies. This is the basis for the Vatican edition of the chant.

The problem of the Gregorian melodies as they existed in the oldest sources was reopened with the publication of the *Antiphonale monasticum* (1932) and the Alemannic *Antiphonale* of the Swiss Benedictine Congregation. The same method of study was used in the publication of the chants of the Milanese liturgy (1936).

CHURCH MUSIC IN THE UNITED STATES

The activities aimed at the reform of church music in the United States were given impetus by the motu proprio. The Liturgical Movement founded and fostered in this country by Dom Virgil Michel of St. John's Abbey, Collegeville, Minnesota, spread into the field of music through the efforts of Dom Gregory Huegle and Dom Ermin Vitry. In 1906, the music-publishing firm of McLaughlin & Reilly was established in Boston, Mass. The Society of St. Gregory of America was formed in June of 1913. This new group, unrelated to the Caecilians, though following the same general aims, brought out its own publication in 1915, *The Catholic Choirmaster*, with Nicola A. Montani as editor. The Society's most far-reaching effort, however, was the publication of the so-called "White List," a catalog of church music considered by its committee to be liturgically acceptable. The "White List" has appeared at frequent intervals since 1928 and, although there is room for debate over its total merit (for its criteria are mainly negative), it has had a decided impact upon music in American churches. Montani in his own right brought about the publication of a new hymnal oriented toward the rising liturgical spirit. This, the *Saint Gregory Hymnal*, was first published in 1921, revised in 1940, and even today is the most widely used hymnbook in the parishes of the United States and English-speaking Canada. Of great importance, too, was a psalm-tone setting of the Mass Propers edited by Carlo Rossini. First published in 1933, and now in its thirteenth edition, it had the distinction of having brought about the singing of the Propers formerly omitted altogether by many parish choirs.

There were also foundations of importance in the educational field in the first quarter of the twentieth century. The School of Liturgical Music of the College of the Sacred Heart, commonly known as the Pius X School, opened its doors on its Manhattanville, N. Y., campus in 1916. The foundresses, Mrs. Justine Ward and Mother Georgia Stevens, helped to propagate the Solesmes method of plain song and to cultivate sacred polyphony. This school is now situated at Purchase, N. Y. In 1953, the school was instrumental in bringing about the publication of a new hymnal, the *Pius X Hymnal.*

Also of value in both the educational and publishing field, the Gregorian Institute of Toledo, Ohio, should be mentioned here.

CHAPTER 17

Contemporary Church Music

THE LITURGICAL MOVEMENT

The motu proprio of St. Pius X (1903), the apostolic constitution of Pius XI (1928), and the encyclical, *Mediator Dei*, of Pius XII (1947) emphasized the significance of church music and its place in the liturgy. The need for a full understanding of the interaction between music and liturgy was underlined by the encyclical, *Musicae sacrae disciplina*, of Pius XII, issued at Christmas, 1955. In the nineteenth century, Prosper Guéranger of Solesmes, Anselm Schott and Maurus Wolter of Beuron, together with Cardinal Wiseman in London, increased appreciation for the dignity and importance of the liturgy. However, it was only after World War I that the Liturgical Movement attained any prominence. It spread into Germany from Belgium where it had begun in 1909 under the direction of Cardinal Mercier and the abbeys of Mont César and Maredsous. A deepening of liturgical understanding took place in Germany, especially at Maria-Laach and Beuron; it was promoted at Klosterneuberg in Austria, and it was brought to life by Romano Guardini, the Leipzig Oratorians and the Rothenfels circle. The whole movement did much to alter the prevailing tradition of church music.

The chant movement, popularized by the abbeys of Gerleve and Grüssau as well as by the youth movement, sought to give the chant its proper place in parochial services and to encourage the active participation of the people in liturgical worship. The song movement for youth (Adam Gottron, Walther Lipphardt) fostered this effort.

The restoration of the traditional Gregorian melodies in the *Editio Vaticana* created the basis for these movements. However, there were various points of view among them. One extreme group wished to establish Gregorian chant as the only music to be used in worship, assigning parts to the chanters, the schola, and the congregation, even though in Christian antiquity and in the Middle Ages musical tasks of this proportion were not expected of the people. Another group wished to include suitable vocal polyphony together with Gregorian chant, suggesting that the Ordinary be assigned to the congregation, while the church choir undertook to provide the Proper in a polyphonic setting. The schola (boys' choir) near the altar sang the special chant parts and thus integrated the music and the sacred action. Christocentric thinking necessarily resulted in a re-evaluation of church music as a whole.

The experiences of World War II and the period preceding have deepened the appreciation of the place of music in worship. No longer can church music be regarded merely as a decorative feature in the service, following its own musical laws; it must be recognized for its artistic genuineness and as a means of liturgical expression. The Liturgical Movement rejected false emotionalism and warned against choking the liturgy with too much music or with musical forms alien to the liturgical spirit.

The Liturgical Movement has endeavored to steer church music back to the liturgical and artistic ideal of medieval worship, and to give back to the congregation an active role in the music of the service. It has attempted to re-create in our own time the ideal music of worship, which has been lost since the Middle Ages. The Liturgical Movement emphasized the artistic unity of a service accompanied exclusively by Gregorian chant, which ties together the singing of the priest, the choir and the people into a single stylistic homogeneity. But to achieve this ideal, a correct and beautiful Gregorian performance is indispensable. This excludes romanticized presentations of the chant, such as occur frequently in actual practice when the pure melody of the chant is wedged into a harmonic setting by the organ accompaniment. Similarly the effort to set the Gregorian melody to vernacular translations that destroy the essential unity of the text and the Gregorian melody must be abandoned.

In combining polyphony with Gregorian chant, the search for artistic unity must be based on the principle of the motu proprio: that a composition is more fitting the closer it comes to Gregorian chant. This is the effort which characterizes modern church music since World War I, when it had to break from the older tradition. The detachment of modern church music, as inspired by the Liturgical Movement, from romantic sentimentalism complements the contemporary artistic development which has changed the emphasis from harmonic elements to melodic lines, from exaggerated external manifestations to real inward expression. The view of the extremists, especially among the youth who sought to exclude all music except Gregorian chant and congregational singing, thus diminishing the liturgical importance of polyphony and the artistic work of the church choir, has been countered by the broad comprehensiveness of the liturgical and artistic views expressed in the papal pronouncements, especially the *Musicae sacrae disciplina* of 1955 and the directives of the Sacred Congregation of Rites of September 3, 1958.

DISAPPEARANCE OF ROMANTICISM

Romanticism of the nineteenth century decayed because of its own excesses of irrational impressionism and realistic naturalism, although some of its aftereffects have persisted into the twentieth century. "Modernized" Caecilianism, and church music in general, remained aloof from this evolution, although in France and Belgium the impressionistic tonal effects gained importance in church music. Julius Van Nuffel (1883–1953) built his great ecclesiastical art on this foundation. Organ music particularly was linked in large measure to impressionism (Marcel Dupré, Flor Peeters), and in turn transferred these tendencies to organ-accompanied church music.

In southern Germany, about the turn of the century, the mild neo-romanticism of Joseph Rheinberger and the full sonorities of Anton Bruckner created new principles for the development of ecclesiastical music. Joseph Renner (1868–1934), Joseph Schmid (b. 1868), Joseph Pembaur (1848–1923) and his son Karl Maria (1876–1939), and others went further in this direction, combining these trends with tonalities in the style of Max Reger and the impressionists. Rooted in romantic conceptions, this art attempted subjective interpretations of the liturgical text and in principle tallied with the new currents of expression that were formed within Caecilianism by Peter Griesbacher, Max Filke, Vincenz Goller, Max Springer, Johannes Georg Meurer, and others. The core of this expressional medium lay in the harmonies and the instrumental accompaniment. Hence in this circle *a cappella* music was replaced by that with organ or orchestral accompaniment. This generation of church composers also included Adalbert Rihovsky, Joseph Kromolicki (b. 1882), and others. They freed church music from its crystallization within traditional forms, and opened the way to ecclesiastical expression in the contemporary idiom.

The music of the early twentieth century continued the expressive forms of the nineteenth century, especially in instrumental music, which often determined the vocal line. Church music so constructed did not fully correspond with the demand of the motu proprio for a vocal music akin to Gregorian chant. The polyphony of the sixteenth century could indeed be imitated, but for the modern period musical development as a whole had not produced an independent *a cappella* style. In the *a cappella* choruses of Bruckner, Rheinberger and Reger a pure vocal melody was developed, but its harmonic foundation and measured rhythm, while making possible a thematic suggestion of Gregorian, did not permit the formation of a free vocal line. After World War I, new liturgical experiences in the spirit of the motu proprio forced church music to develop an *a cappella* art. These efforts were aligned with emphasis on the melodic line which appeared in the general evolution of music, permitting the development of a melody freed from the restrictions of harmony. This linear interest first appeared in the string quartet, but it found its perfect vocal character in church music. The ecclesiastical vocal polyphony of Joseph Haas (1879–1960) in Munich and Heinrich Lemacher (b. 1891) in Cologne expressed a new experience in art and liturgy that led vocal music to a distinctive manner of expression.

The emphasis on distinctly vocal expression influenced also the music conceived on harmonic foundations and with instrumental accompaniment. It was felt by composers of varying backgrounds. This is most clearly seen in the later work of Joseph Venantius von Wöss. Coming from the Bruckner circle, Wöss was affected by the Liturgical Movement and produced a rich vocal expression, among the most advanced in modern church music. The same was true of Joseph Lechthaler (1891–1948) around whom a circle of modern Viennese church musicians was formed. A distinctive motion of the vocal melodic lines overcame a rhythm that was heavily dependent upon even measure and a harmony that formerly dictated the voice leading. Thus a linear form of expression gave meaning to the liturgical phrase. This evolution was free from the tonal abstraction seen in the more extreme examples of linear writing and in attempts at restoration of the ancient polyphony. It is likewise linked to another evolution that intermingles linear polyphony and harmony as seen in the works of composers who wrote primarily for instruments. Among them are Joseph Messner (b. 1893), Otto Siegl (b. 1896), Carl Senn, Karl Kraft (b. 1903), Heinrich Kaspar Schmid (1874–1953), Arthur Piechler (b. 1898), Otto Jochum (b. 1898), Ludwig Berberich (b. 1882), Christoph Lorenz Kagerer (b. 1886), Leo Söhner (1898–1954), Ernst Tittel (b. 1910), Johann Hafner (b. 1901), and Hermann Wunsch (1884–1954). Amid many harmonic and melodic adjustments, the voice line takes the lead. Vocal polyphony also dominates the accompaniment which lends the liturgical phrase an inward musical meaning in the spirit of individualistic piety. This basic attitude of the Austrian and south German composers is not very different from that of the Silesian church musicians. Of these, Hermann Buchal (b. 1884), Gerhard Strecke (b. 1890), Victor Friedrich (b. 1904), Franz Kauf (b. 1883), Alfred Töpler (b. 1883), Artur Wittek (b. 1892), Paul Blaschke (b. 1885), P. J. Kobeck, and others have written works worthy of special attention.

MODERN CHURCH MUSIC IN GERMANY

"Expression instead of pathos," "authenticity instead of unreal make-believe" became bywords in every area of artistic life during the second decade of the twentieth century. Expressionism apparently had to break with every tradition of musical style. In close kinship with the Gothic spirit it shaped the artistic speech of the times in many different ways. Church music in its liturgical consciousness was wholly alien to the pathos of romanticism and its intrinsic disintegration in the works of Arnold Schönberg (1874–1951). Alien as well to naturalism and impressionism, musicians found in expressionism an area where it was possible to build a rapport between church music and the general evolution of music. Linear construction is essential to polyphonic voice linking. Similarly melodic expression, free from harmonic or agogic interpretation, is the foundation of the music form sought for the liturgy. If the linear polyphony of Paul Hindemith (b. 1895), Ernst Krenek (b. 1900), and Anton von Webern (1883–1945) is considered novel in harmony and structure, in principle it points back to the art of the early Netherland school of the fifteenth century, the starting-point for a great evolution in ecclesiastical vocal polyphony. In the course of the fourteenth and fifteenth centuries the weightless undulation of the Gregorian melody had been linked to an equalized time value. A similar break with tradition today, by emphasizing a linear treatment of melody, has unshackled itself to create a new means of expression. Hermann Erpf (b. 1891) has brought this latest borrowing of a nonharmonic Gregorian melody into reality in his *Mass for One Voice*, but borrowed melodies of this sort have obtained more importance in later Lutheran music than in Catholic. Ernst Pepping (b. 1901), Hugo Distler (1908–1942), Heinrich Kaminski (1886–1946), and others shaped them into a harmonic consonance. In Catholic church music, Marius Monnikendam (b. 1896), Kaspar Roeseling (1894–1960) and Ludwig Weber (1891–1947) have been the most radical in giving reality and liturgical expression to these linear melodies. Freed tonally from every tradition of harmonic relationship, this art with its Gregorian melody is alien to any functional harmony. As in the style of the fourteenth and fifteenth centuries, vertical relationship in the harmony is achieved by means of parallel sounds, faux-bourdon and cadential formations. The fourth and fifth replace the third as the prevalent consonants. The contrapuntal leading of the voices is accomplished by means of strict imitation, and by parallel and contrary motion in the style of the early Netherlanders. Free of any harmonic demands, the linear melodies produce sharp clashes of dissonance. This complete etherialization of art resulted in a withdrawal from the text. Although this was in accordance with a very strict conception of liturgy, it necessarily implied a complete break with the traditional conception of church music and its use of harmonic devices. Linear expressionism brought about the use of Gregorian melody free from harmonic considerations, and so gave rise to a polyphony that corresponded to the demands of the motu proprio.

But the mystery of the liturgy had become estranged from homocentric Western thought since the Renaissance, and its revival was grasped only in small circles and there perhaps only externally. Thus this extreme answer of abstract expression could not obtain any wide acceptance in church music in view of the sensuousness of every other musical experience of the era. Similar to the extreme spiritual trends of music in the Gothic era, this abstract expressionism was drawn again into the boundaries of tonal perceptiveness.

In the second decade of the twentieth century, ecclesiastical vocal polyphony gained a new and distinctive character with Joseph Haas in Munich and Heinrich Lemacher in Cologne. Starting with the contrapuntalism of Max Reger, Haas gave the *a cappella* technique in his *German Mass* and *Vespers* a new trend-making form in expression and sound. In his canonic motets, linear freedom reached its highest levels. In a rich display of ecclesiastical compositions, Heinrich Lemacher also used the new tonal language to produce a strict ecclesiastical *a cappella* style, a new form of expression that had the most telling effect on his numerous students. Building on Gregorian themes, he shaped the free choral sweep of his voice relationships into a profoundly liturgical expression. It was functionless harmony in a combination of sounds not unlike organum and faux-bourdon of the Gothic era but similar to the harmonic tensions of tone clusters. Active in Munich along with Joseph Haas was Gottfried Rüdinger (1886–1946), with his cleverly elaborated style and his profoundly conceived church music. Karl Kraft (b. 1863), Arthur Piechler (b. 1898), Otto Jochum (b. 1898), Leo Söhner (b. 1898), Heinrich Wismeyer, Max Jobst (1908–1943), Hans Gebhard (b. 1897), Joseph Sell (b. 1901), Hans Lang (b. 1897), and Adolf Pfanner (b. 1897), have cultivated the liturgical style of expression to some extent in connection with instrumental sonority. Numerous south-German, Austrian and Swiss composers approach the basic stylistic attitude of the Munich group. Outstanding among them, with works of rich sonority, are Hugo Herrmann (b. 1896) and Franz Philipp (b. 1890) of Baden, while the Swiss, Johann Baptist Hilber (b. 1891), is more akin to the Cologne group. The new church music had a special development among Rhenish church composers. Theodore B. Rehmann's expressive and rich compositions are created in the spirit of a perfected choral art. Although in Theodor Pfeiffer (b. 1875), Johann Josef Veith (b. 1872), Anton Knüppel (b. 1880) and Wilhelm Kurthen (1882–1957) links with the older style are still at work, Franz Josef Wagner-Cochem, Heinrich Weber, Bernhard Hartmann (b. 1892) and Kaspar Roeseling (1894–1960) approach the newer sounds. The strongest expression, however, is achieved by Hermann Schroeder (b. 1902), in whose liturgical music and other religious compositions linear treatment of the melody produces a particularly rich and powerful sonority. The Danish priest, Leif Keyser, shows the same bent towards a linear profile in his composition.

In the masses of Joseph Ahrens (b. 1904) of Berlin, the spirit of Gregorian chant has been grandly invested in a modern tonal language. Hans Marie Dombrowski (b. 1897), Theodor Pröpper (b. 1896), Herbert Marx (b. 1903), and others have produced some little works of church music in modern tonal language. Hajo Kelling (b. 1907), Alfred Berghorn (b. 1911), and Heino Schubert (b. 1928), although strongly rooted in tradition, also emphasize the contemporary style with its novel tonalities.

The new expression touched all forms of ecclesiastical music. Since the Liturgical Movement urged the singing of the Ordinary of the Mass in Gregorian chant, a special impetus was given the composition of music for the proper parts. Noteworthy are the settings of Otto Jochum and Heinrich Lemacher. New devotional songs in choral collections have been published along with liturgical music. The combination of the congregation, the choir and the soloist has introduced many new possibilities. Finally, with the use of wind instruments in connection with the choir, present-day church music has attained fresh tonal horizons.

The emphasis on linear construction in modern church music, using the Gregorian melodies free of any harmonic background, differs from the treatment given the chant melodies in the ancient classical polyphony where the counterpoint of the voices produced an harmonically conceived sonority. The centuries following the great achievement of Renaissance polyphony utilized this development to the fullest. By putting the Gregorian themes into a harmonic context, one school of modern composition builds on the old polyphonic technique. This neo-Palestrinan style is strictly diatonic, but it employs modern harmony. It is not a mere imitation, because it achieves a personal expression of the meaning of the texts. It is actually the art that Caecilianism was seeking but did not discover. K. Thiel (1862–1942), Wilhelm Kurthen (b. 1882), and Raffaele Casimiri (1880–1943) employed their historical knowledge to make the ancient classical polyphony the basis of their liturgical music, in accordance with the stress laid on the Palestrinan style in the motu proprio. Alfons Schlögl (1886–1926) and Thomas Hagedorn sought to strengthen this expression by expanding the harmonic palette, as did Franz Stockhausen, Clemens von Droste, P. Blaschke (b. 1885) and Gunther Bialas. Kurt Doebler (b. 1896), however, gave the strict contrapuntal melodic structure of Palestrina a new shape by a rich change of tonality and thus made it the support of a new mode of expression.

Proceeding from its own essential form and spirit, but on a modern basis, the Palestrinan style has thus attained importance in modern church music and taken its place alongside the forms of contemporary church music based on Gregorian chant. Like the development of music in general, the great advance of liturgical music in the newly discovered stylistic world of the second decade of the twentieth century was gradually clarified and established in its basic position, and soon reached a balance between schools that at first were sharply divided.

NEW CURRENTS IN OTHER EUROPEAN COUNTRIES

The *rapprochement* between church music and other contemporary arts, brought about in Germany by a deepening of interest in the liturgy, was duplicated in other countries. Following in the currents of musical progress in the West, composers of Belgium and the Netherlands have constructed a church music similar to that produced in the nearby Rhineland. Arthur Meulemans (b. 1884), R. Herberigs (b. 1886), Jef van Hoof (b. 1886), Louis de Vocht, Julius van Nuffel (1883–1953), Johann Winnubst (1885–1924), Hendrik Andriessen (b. 1892), Marinus de Jong, Jaap Vranken and Flor Peeters (b. 1903) have found their liturgical expression in a linear melodic structure linked to tonality. While bowing to the traditions of the past, this music inclines more toward impressionism by avoiding functional harmony and emphasizing linear construction. Alfons Diepenbrock (1862–1921) brought Holland's church music up to date, but Marius Monnikendam (b. 1896), after World War I, made the strongest break with tradition. Other Dutch composers deserve to be mentioned here, among them Hermann Strategier (b. 1912), Jan Mul (b. 1911), Albert de Klerk (b. 1917), and Jan Nieland. In Belgium the link to the tonal riches of impressionism continued to be strong, but its rhythmical refinements were perfected, especially by Van Nuffel.

Following the lead of Bela Bartok (1881–1945), whose inspiration was found in folk songs, Hungarian composers have become prominent through the use of new tonal techniques in solving the problem of expression. Dezsö Démenyi (1878–1937) and Bardos (b. 1899) have achieved an original form for their art, and Zoltan Kodàly (b. 1882) has injected into his ecclesiastical compositions a note of traditional Magyar music but in a wholly contemporary tonality. His example has been followed by a pupil of his, Lajos Bardos.

Austrian church music has remained, in general, more traditional, but Josef F. Doppelbauer (b. 1918) discreetly welds tradition and progress into a fine modern style. Karl Walter (1892–1959), Franz Krieg (b. 1898), and Hans Bauernfeind (b. 1908) combine a warm Austrian indivi˙ ˙˙

with a firm understanding of vocal technique. Other Austrian composers of note include Hermann Kronsteiner (b. 1914), Joseph Kronsteiner, Anton Heiller (b. 1923), and Ernst Tittel (b. 1910).

In France, religious music moved closer to contemporary art, but actual service music continued to adhere in the main to an artless tradition and to the romantic past. However, new impulses have come from the spiritual music that was itself prompted by romanticism and impressionism. The subjective, dramatic church music of Jules Massenet (1842–1912) and Camille Saint-Saëns (1835–1921) was a great influence on Charles Bordes (1863–1909), Gabriel Fauré (1845–1921), Vincent d'Indy (1851–1931), Charles Widor (1845–1907), Louis Vierne (1870–1937), Leon Saint-Requier (b. 1872), A. Alcain (b. 1880), Amédée Gastoué (1873–1943), Fernand de la Tombelle, Alexis de Castillon (1838–1873), Joseph Marie Erb (1860–1944), and others. This is proof of the ties that bind French church music to the past. Only a few composers, including André Caplet (1879–1925), have found their way to a linear, melodic construction, although influenced to a degree by impressionistic sonorities. Charles Koechlin (1867–1951), Theodore Dubois (1837–1924), Albert Bertelin (1872–1951), Guy Ropartz (1864–1935) and Henri Potiron (b. 1882) have gone their own ways along these lines. Jean Langlais has developed a style that combines the traits of impressionism with a stark modal technique. The Schola Cantorum, center of liturgical music in France, has remained linked to a church music hidebound by tradition.

Two contrasting currents exist in French church music. For one, the Gregorian chant holds first place, backed by the severe interpretation of Solesmes. Its chief creativity has been in the composition of harmonic accompaniments, such as those of Henri Potiron and others, or in the thematic elaboration of Gregorian motifs. The other group has produced only shallow *cantiques*, solo or choral compositions with instrumental accompaniment. Much modern composition has not observed the liturgical restrictions and has incorporated strange effects that often lack true appreciation of the liturgical spirit. In contrast to Germany where the new tonal language grew from a Gregorian style into a polyphonic form, the new technique in France was adapted simply to extraliturgical, religious music. It was an influence on church music, but Gregorian chant was employed only as an extrinsic theme.

Church music conditions in Spain are much the same. Expressionism has not led to any new developments. Nemesio Otanio (1880–1956), J. Prieto

(b. 1900) and others continued within the bounds of the old tradition, linking the ancient polyphony and superimposed impressionistic harmonic effects. Spanish church music is especially preoccupied with Gregorian chant and the tradition of polyphony.

In England, too, the conditions for the development of a new church music have hardly been favorable. Modern expression, however, did influence Charles Wood (1866–1926), Vaughan Williams (1872–1958), Herbert Howells (b. 1892) and G. Oldroyd (b. 1886). Richard Terry (1865–1938), L. Long and others were assiduous in cultivating both ancient and modern church music.

The Italians were important in the development of the new expression in church music. Just as in France, religious music in general accepted contemporary techniques which thus exerted great influences on church music. The effect of impressionism was especially strong, particularly in the work of Lorenzo Perosi (1872–1956). Ildebrando Pizzetti (b. 1880), Eduardo Dagnino (b. 1876), Adolfo Bossi (1876–1953), Ottorino Respighi (1879–1936), Licinio Refice, Giulio Bas (1874–1929), Giorgio Federico Ghedini (b. 1892), and Ettore Desderi (b. 1892) cultivated modern church music. While impressionism in harmony is generally predominant, Ghedini and Desderi employed linear writing effectively. With this means Desderi produced *a cappella* settings with the clarity of Palestrina. Domenico Bartolucci (b. 1917) presents a modern adaptation of sixteenth century polyphonic techniques. Bonaventura Somma, on the other hand, has created a new style based on the warm melodic tradition of Italian song but combined with a modern harmonic treatment.

The peculiar turn in the development of church music in the Romance countries had its effect also in western Switzerland. Joseph Bovet (1879–1951), William Montillet (b. 1879), and O. A. Tichy (b. 1890) have striven for new expression in church music. The supporters of contemporary church music in German-speaking Switzerland are especially Joseph Müller, Johann Baptist Hilber (b. 1891), Oswald Jaeggi, and A. Jenny. On the other hand Casimir Meister (b. 1869), Josef Heinrich Dietrich, Josef Frei, Otto Rehm, Josef Scheel (1879–1943), holding closer to tradition, have carried on the fruitful work of J. Y. E. Stehle (1839–1915) in many noteworthy compositions.

In Jugoslavia the new art of Emil Hochreiter stands in contrast to the traditional church music of Anton Foerster (1837–1926), P. Hugolin Sattner (1851–1934), Stanislaus Premrl and Franz Kimovec.

CONTEMPORARY CHURCH MUSIC IN THE UNITED STATES

Since World War II many more institutions of higher learning in the United States have set up specific curricula for degrees in church music. The Catholic University of America in Washington, De Paul University of Chicago, and Alverno College of Milwaukee are among the leaders in this movement. In addition many convents and seminaries have incorporated programs of training in church music for aspirants to the priesthood and the sisterhood. Workshops lasting two weeks or more are conducted for organists and choirmasters; one of the most important of these, employing a staff of world-renowned musicians and liturgists, is held each year at Boys Town, Nebraska. The National Catholic Music Educators Association helps foster methods for introducing music of artistic probity, both sacred and secular, to the parochial school children.

Shortly after World War II, Omer Westendorf, a choirmaster in Cincinnati, founded the World Library of Sacred Music, at first in the main a distributing house for church music published in Europe, but later a publishing house in its own right, encouraging new creative talent in the United States. The World Library has published the *People's Hymnal* for the specific use of congregations, and has led the field in the publication of materials for participation in the Mass. Other firms are also doing much to foster popular participation, notably the Liturgical Press of St. John's Abbey, Collegeville, Minnesota, which publishes *Worship*, a periodical devoted to the liturgical apostolate.

The final test of the profundity inherent in any musical movement is, however, the number and excellence of composers arising out of an artistic soil conditioned by sufficient background and by public acceptance. On this score the United States is beginning to emerge as a center for church-music composition. One can only list some of the many composers of influence and indicate their basic musical idiom. The strict Caecilianism of John Singenberger and his school has been succeeded by other and more modern currents. Ludwig Bonvin (1849–1939), A. Rhode, and Elmer Andrew Steffen show affinities to the German Caecilians, while Pietro A. Yon (1886–1943), Carlo Rossini (b. 1890) and Nicola A. Montani (1880–1948) are linked to the Italian manner. A strict conservatism also characterizes the work of J. Alfred Schehl (1882–1959) and Sr. M. Cherubim (b. 1886). A traditional idiom is also characteristic of the works of Cyr de Brant (J. V. Higginson), Joseph J. McGrath,

210

Richard K. Biggs, P. C. Tonner and others. Less conservative but still traditional are such writers as Philip G. Kreckel, Camille Van Hulse, Theodore Marier, Laurence Powell, Roger Wagner, Achile P. Bragers, Frank Campbell-Watson, and Sr. M. Theophane. Some of these employ the Gregorian modal idioms or incorporate Gregorian themes into a free polyphonic style, and in fact Bragers is perhaps best known for his organ accompaniments to the chant. Kreckel, Van Hulse, Schehl, Sr. M. Theophane and Mario Salvador must be mentioned for their excellent work and craftsmanship in the field of organ composition. However, in organ music it is the development in non-Catholic religious groups that continues to exercise the greatest influence; Seth Bingham, Leo Sowerby, Everett Titcomb, and Healy Willan have a considerable effect on Catholic church music.

There is a growing body of composers who have been influenced by the more revolutionary techniques of Europe. These men include Paul Creston, Noel Goemanne, Louis Huybrechts, John Larkin, C. Alexander Peloquin and Russell Woollen. Woollen perhaps has developed the most highly individual style in this starkly dissonant idiom. Max Seeboth and Ernst Krenek are both composing in the United States. It would be very negligent to omit mention of such distinguished composers as the Canadian Healy Willan who, although not a Catholic, has written some of the most profoundly beautiful organ and choral music of our day, much of it usable in the Catholic liturgy. Joseph Roff, also from Canada, and Julian Zuñiga, the Mexican composer, must also be mentioned, as well as Hector Villa-Lobos (1881–1959) of Brazil.

EXTRALITURGICAL AND OTHER RELIGIOUS MUSIC

The liturgical function of church music has had the effect of circumscribing it and at the same time of influencing devotional music for extraliturgical services. In Germany, especially, there has been considerable activity in vernacular hymnody as well as in the composition of motets, litanies, etc. The same interest in hymns in the vernacular has stirred other countries, notably Holland and the United States, and the program for popular participation in the liturgy, especially in France, has increased activity in the composition of so-called "people's masses" and aroused interest in vernacular forms, especially the psalms.

As with liturgical music various stylistic groups appear here too. Especially in evidence is the subjective interpretation of the text. Thus Julius Bittner and Walter Braunfels (1882–1954) set the liturgical texts so elaborately that they exceeded the liturgical restrictions. But the distinctive qualities of this tendency are seen most clearly in the church cantata and in the solo or multivoiced devotional hymn, where sacred song has had the greatest chance for development in extraliturgical devotions. Joseph Haas, Gottfried Rüdinger, Heinrich Lemacher, Hermann Schroeder, Johann Baptist Hilber, Otto Jochum and others have created such works either in well-conceived cycles or as individual pieces. Julius van Nuffel's mighty psalms, Jaap Vranken's tuneful songs, Flor Peeters' expressive religious works, and Bardo's imaginative compositions are among the many works in this direction that can be mentioned.

Not all religious music is intended for liturgical or extraliturgical services. It is rather a part of musical life as a whole. Until after World War I religious music was largely influenced by secular music, at least in the larger forms. However, it has now found a source for new inspiration in the latest developments of church music. In Italy Lorenzo Perosi's religious oratorios were closely linked with liturgical·music. Licinio Refice, Gian Francesco Malipiero and others, in their cantatas and oratorios, developed this same spirit. Even instrumental music, nonexistent as a means of sacred expression since the days of the church sonata and the religious *concerto grosso* of the seventeenth century, has attained a spiritual depth in the writings of Ottorino Respighi, Refice and Malipiero. Gregorian themes and the Gregorian spirit have invaded instrumental music and opened to it a world hitherto generally barred. In Germany Karl Höller and Hermann Schroeder have given shape to this type of expression in their orchestral hymns. Joseph Haas used it in his religious oratories, especially in his so-called "popular oratorio" in which he bridged the gap between podium and audience by means of community singing. In his opera *Tobias Wunderlich*, the musical form is permeated by the spirit of religious experience. Hugo Herrmann, Franz Philipp, and others have given new life and new magnitude to the religious oratorio. The massing of choruses in Ludwig Weber's work has had its influence not only on religious music in general but on church music as well.

In France men like Darius Milhaud (b. 1892), Arthur Honegger (1892–1956) and Igor Stravinski (b. 1882) have opened up a new world of religious expression by their use of psalms and other sacred texts in new musical forms. Albert Rousel (1869–1937), Henri Rabaud (1873–1949), Guy Ropartz (1864–1935), and Florent Schmitt (1870–1955) also contributed to religious music by their work. Rivier, Manuel Rosenthal, Damais, Charles Séringes, Georges Migot and Olivier Messiaen have done their greatest work in the field of religious music. In 1924, André Caplet's (1879–1925) *Miroir de Jesus* and Honegger's *Roi David* gave France's new religious music a most distinctive character, continuing the evolution of César Franck, Camille Saint-Saëns, Jules Massenet, Vincent d'Indy and Gabriel Pierné (1863–1937). Albert Bertelin (b. 1872), Vadon, Charles Koechlin (b. 1867) and F. Brun have all created great religious works in the second and third decade of the twentieth century. In fact it should be said that religious music has achieved an important place in contemporary French musical life.

Similarly Polish composers like Karol Szymanowski (1883–1937), Felix Nowowiewski (b. 1877) and Lucian Kamienski (b. 1885) have created important works in the new religious mold.

Besides the larger contemporary religious works, all countries have produced religious chamber music in various forms. Contemporary expression has given it new shape and depth by linear and impressionistic tonal effects. There is also religious piano music for two and four hands by Ottorino Respighi, Kaspar Roeseling, Heinrich Lemacher, and Hermann Schroeder. Roeseling and his group created new types of religious music for children.

PEOPLE'S SONG

The liturgical movement gave new impetus to the activation of the congregation in worship. According to ancient tradition the acclamations had always belonged to the people and the effort was made to restore these to them. An effort was also made to combine congregational participation with polyphony, especially in the composition of masses with sections set aside for the people. Masses by Franz Xavier Matthias, Josef G. Scheel, and others, and more recently those by Ernst Tittel, W. Waldbroel, and Hermann Schroeder combine part music with unison sections for the congregation. Unison masses also served the same purpose.

The greatest development in music for the congregation took place in the vernacular hymn. In Germany, hymnbooks still contain a preponderance of older hymns and many by composers of the Caecilian school, with sentimental pieces from the period of the Enlightenment. Efforts made since 1908 to introduce a unified collection for the whole of Germany were for the most part blocked by local and diocesan traditions. But the problem has grown with the shifts in population caused by the two World Wars. Still little agreement has been reached, except on less than a hundred hymns. It is a repetition of the story of liturgical unity sought in the sixteenth century. Preference for local traditions overrode the desire for uniformity. It was not until the introduction of the *Editio Vaticana* that vestiges of local variants in the chant were finally eradicated. Such a break with beloved tradition is indeed to be regretted, although good local forms can often be retained along with the unified hymnal. The needs of the times will best be served by a greater use of old tunes long forgotten as well as contemporary hymns that have not as yet been included in many hymnbooks. Church music has advanced since the age of the Caecilians and the hymnals of Joseph Kreitmaier. In the vernacular mass composed for the cathedral of Speyer, and in his other *Singmessen*, Joseph Haas has brought liturgical piety into the hymn. The same line was followed by the popular German masses of J. Alt, Arthur Piechler, Karl Kraft, Gottfried Rüdinger, Carl Frey, Vincenz Goller, Christian Lahusen, F. Weidmann, Max Jobst, Josef Lechthaler, Clausing, Erhard Quack, and others. Youth societies have contributed to hymnody both by the revival of worthwhile old hymns and the introduction of new ones by A. Lohmann, H. Neuss, Rohr and others. The basis for this work was the research into the original texts and melodies of ancient hymns, as was done especially by Hermann Müller (1868–1932) and J. Gotzen (b. 1875). In this problem of the hymn as in other problems of church music, Johannes Hatzfeld has proved himself the discoverer and promoter of old and new. Valuable contributions to the dominant question of the union of text and melody are found in the writings of Gerhard Strecke, Theodor Pröpper, Franz Philipp, J. Discher and others. Various kinds of devotional hymns have been composed by Joseph Haas, Gottfried Rüdinger, Heinrich Lemacher, Franz Philipp and others. Their solution of the problem of hymnody is a deft combination of the traditional music of the people with what is genuinely artistic in the modern vein.

Holland, too, has had a resurgence of interest in hymnody in the vernacular. Marinus de Jong, Hermann Strategier, Hendrik Andriessen, and Jan Nieland are among those working in this special field.

In France the vernacular *cantiques* are widely used. But during the 1920s a reawakened liturgical awareness occasioned a violent controversy over sentimental traditional hymns as contrasted with those based on Gregorian melodies. With his collection of Gregorian hymns F. Brun hoped to replace the trashy and often worldly melodies to which French texts were set. Similarly Vincent d'Indy created Gregorian-type hymns, and Guy de Lioncourt mixed modern and Gregorian melodies. Dévdat de Sévérac, Charles Bordes and others also worked to put greater depth into the hymn, but the stubborn traditions have not yielded easily.

Similar problems plague Spanish hymnody. Since the second decade of our century N. Otanio and others have tried to add better hymns. The Liturgical Movement has had the same effect everywhere in uprooting the pietistic trumpery that goes by the name of tradition. In Poland and Hungary the hymn problem has been fought by the revival of ancient hymns and by the promotion of Gregorian chant.

THE ORGAN AND ORGAN PLAYING

The twentieth century has witnessed a spirited revival of the art of organ construction as well as organ playing. Shortly after World War I artists like Albert Schweitzer, E. Rupp and Franz Xaver Mathias reawakened interest in the historical sound of the organ of the Bach period, in contradistinction to the sounds proper to the orchestralike organ that had been developed in the nineteenth century. About the same time Willibald Gurlitt instituted a movement to restore the tonal ideal of the Praetorius organ and to evaluate organ tones through historical research. Even organ playing had a historical revival, with Karl Straube and Günther Ramin insisting on the interpretation of ancient masters, especially Bach, according to historical tonal ideals.

Naturally organ construction and organ playing in the Catholic Church were affected by these movements. Organ playing within the liturgy demanded a tonal quality somewhere between the historical type of the Praetorius and Silbermann organs and that of the contemporary organ. In countless constructions and remodelings a new special tone was developed suited to the presentation both of the old music and the contemporary.

Since Rheinberger, César Franck and Enrico Bossi, church organ music has taken a decided upward leap. Max Reger (1873–1916) broadened the form and expression of organ music in forceful polyphony and harmony, bringing it to monumental proportions. The predominantly contrapuntal character of his work, modeled on Bach, stands in marked contrast to the tone colors of the French organ symphonies of Charles

Widor (1845–1947), Alexandre Guilmant (1837–1911), and Louis Vierne (1870–1937), who sought for impressionistic tonal effects. For Charles Tournemire (1870–1939), Marcel Dupré (b. 1886), Joseph Bonnet, Menalt, Maurice Duruflé, Bermal, Olivier Messiaen, Jean Langlais, Paul Benoit and a host of modern French organists impressionism was the stylistic principle. In versets, ecclesiastical character-pieces and thematic elaborations of Gregorian chants, contemporary French organ music strives to furnish an assistance to worship. The mixture of Bach's structure with impressionistic tonal effects is the special note of this type of music. Flor Peeters, in Belgium, has contributed notable organ works along this line.

In striking contrast to the tone-conscious Romance countries, organ music in Germany pursued structural and linear tendencies based on the strict contrapuntal forms of the seventeenth and eighteenth centuries, with their clean lines and balance. Johann Nepomuk David, Hermann Schroeder, Joseph Ahrens, Heinrich Weber, Kurt Doebler, and Josef Lechthaler are among the Catholic musicians writing this type of organ music. The Gregorian theme usually controls the work which is cast in one of the many forms of the Baroque period. Georg Trexler in his Gregorian organ compositions has been especially successful in producing a modern organ art with liturgical melodies.

This linear tendency in independent organ composition has affected organ accompaniment and freed it from its strictly chordal-harmonic forms. In the modern organ masses of Rheinberger, for example, the organ accompaniment is attached contrapuntally to the voice part and thus acquires structural significance.

The accompaniment of Gregorian chant has also experienced various changes. From a purely harmonic conception with diatonic chords Griesbacher passed to a chromatic style far removed from the chant modes. In the latest developments the free movement of the Gregorian *melos* has led to a linear treatment of the organ accompaniment. Giulio Bas, Henri Potiron, Peter Wagner, and later Herbert Desrocquettes and Achille Bragers, introduced the passing note and suspension. In his chant accompaniments Julius van Nuffel achieved a compromise between ancient organum and faux-bourdon on the one hand and linear construction and functional harmony on the other. However, on historical and stylistic grounds, an increasing number rejected any accompaniment whatsoever. This encouraged the writing of versets, long a part of the functional church music of the Romance countries. They were used in conjunction with the unaccompanied chant. Improvisation, using the themes of the various sung parts of the service, has found new life by employing contrapuntal techniques in place of restricted, cadential harmonies. This ancient art has been revived by such outstanding artists and composers as Marcel Dupré, Flor Peeters, H. Bachem, J. Stollenwerk, Hermann Schroeder, Joseph Ahrens and others.

CHURCH MUSIC ORGANIZATIONS

Many organizations were formed to promote good music. In the nineteenth century, the Caecilian societies in Germany, Italy, and elsewhere did much for the church music movement. Similar organizations, including the Society of St. Gregory in the United States, served to implement the ordinances of the motu proprio of St. Pius X. Other organizations, for example in the field of education the National Catholic Music Educators Association, have sought to inculcate an understanding and appreciation of good church music as a cultural medium.

One event in the twentieth century is of particular significance, not merely for the culture of one country, but for the church universal. This was the founding in 1927 at Frankfort on the Main of the International Society for the Renewal of Church Music (IGK). While the Caecilian societies are concerned with the spread of good music in every area of church life, the IGK has for its aim the cultivation of the newer styles and their spread into the religious life of the world at large. Its conventions have presented a broad view of the creative genius of the modern religious composers of many countries. It fosters the production of new music, not merely because it is modern, but in order to fill the liturgical and religious needs of the modern world. The IGK, in a sense, is a composer's organization, aimed at welding the writers of the day into a coöperative unit. Johann Hatzfeld was the successful promoter of the ideals of the IGK, and Joseph Haas was for years the organizing and guiding hand. After World War II the IGK affiliated with the Caecilian Society in German-speaking countries. A new world-wide organization of Catholic Church musicians was founded in 1961, as a result of the International Congresses of Church Music at Rome (1950), Vienna, Paris and Cologne, which will connect the different national Societies of Catholic Church Music.

THE FUTURE

The twentieth century, after two World Wars, has witnessed a remarkable revival of interest in church music. Much has been done to promote its better performance. Everywhere new schools have been founded or reactivated to foster a deeper knowledge of the music of the past and to train musicians for the present. The Pontifical Institute of Sacred Music in Rome, founded in 1911, is an indication of the value the Holy See puts on the training of musicians and the fostering of art in the church. Its president, Monsignor Higini Anglès, is widely known as a teacher and musicologist. The scientific work of other scholars including Otto Ursprung, Wilhelm Kurthen, Arnold Schmitz, J. Schmidt-Görg, Amédée Gastoué, Raffaele Casimiri, and others has done much to clarify the understanding of older church music and prepare it for practical use. There is still much to be done, because so much of the great choral work of the fifteenth, sixteenth, and seventeenth centuries still awaits publication in practical editions.

Gregorian chant, too, has been studied assiduously. The research into manuscripts and ancient documents made by Peter Wagner, André Mocquereau, Gregorio Suñol, Paolo Ferretti, Dominic Johner, Michel Huglo, Bruno Stäblein, and others has given valuable insights into the performance of liturgical music. All the problems are not settled. Questions of rhythm, melodic forms and performance practice must be studied and solved.

All this augurs well for the future. The tremendous material losses suffered by Europe in two World Wars were counterbalanced by a remarkable recovery of the cultural spirit and the acquisition of a deeper sense of the liturgy. Coupled with a greater knowledge of the Gregorian tradition and the treasures of ancient classical polyphony, this resurgence of the ecclesiastical spirit has renewed interest in attaining the ideal setting for actual performance. The accomplishment of the directives of the motu proprio and of other documents of the Holy See must become more than a dream. This is the real work of the future.

It is always the task of liturgical music to achieve a proper correlation of text and music and to put this in the service of worship. A primary duty is the training of choirs, especially for the performance of the chant, whether this be the *cantus accentus* (simple chant) or the *cantus concentus* (ornate chant). Both forms demand an appreciation of the word-tone

218

relationship and a knowledge of tone production as keen as is necessary in polyphony and modern harmony.

The artistic realization of liturgical thought in tone must take shape creatively as an expression of our own time. In some instances this may entail a break with traditions that have become mere relics devoid of any power to produce liturgical experience, or it may even demand new forms of expression. Liturgy and church music cannot just stand side by side; they must interpenetrate. Only what is artistically the best can be good enough for worship. It is along such lines that the future task of church music will be found, and no doubt many solutions will be discovered for the problems involved. Man today, surrounded by a great artistic culture, is perhaps more critical in his musical tastes than were earlier generations. Radio, television, and recordings bring him the very best in choral and instrumental music. If church music is to fulfill its liturgical and artistic task, it must take cognizance of the fact that good intentions are not enough. It will realize its end only in a spiritual alliance between the church and culture. Both the composition and the performance of church music must meet these high standards.

New forms of music for worship will necessarily appear alongside revitalized old ones. Active participation of the people is a special problem. Its solution remains to be seen. Obviously, however, there must be a creative ingenuity coming from the spirit and text of the liturgy, so that eloquence and music are joined in a sincere expression of the age. New hymns must take a place beside old ones that are good and replace those that are sentimental and superficial. Gregorian chant, bound as it is to a Latin text, must be made something living to display its liturgical and artistic power. A re-apportionment of the choral parts of the mass to various singing groups, including the congregation, has already produced musical results in the creation of various masses for choir and people. Similar possibilities present themselves for vernacular singing, drawing together the choir and the congregation. For the organist there is a real opportunity, by means of thematic preludes and postludes, to re-create an art that has for the most part gone unused since the eighteenth century.

Pius XII pointed up another challenge for the church musician of today in extraliturgical religious music, which he describes as "a powerful aid to religion." In the spirit of St. Philip Neri (1515–1594), the work of providing contact between the church and the world must embrace all the arts, especially in view of the progress in radio, television, motion pictures, and recording techniques. In these media many problems arise

for the church musician. In radio and television productions of church
services, the question of content and artistic framing must be answered.
Is it sufficient merely to transmit the live program without adjustment,
or should the new medium condition the forms to be used, especially the
music? The oratorio and the opera were neglected as religious forms
during the nineteenth century, but at the present they are making a come-
back under the competent hands of composers including Joseph Haas,
Franz Philipp, and others. Similarly the religious drama, the mystery
play, and other theatrical forms present new challenges for the composer
of sacred music.

The destruction of so many churches and organs during World War
II, with subsequent scarcity of materials for rebuilding, stimulated composers to explore new musical forms that might fulfill the liturgical and
artistic requirements even under the humblest conditions. The encyclical,
Musicae sacrae disciplina, with its more tolerant view of the use of strings
and wind instruments, was an official invitation to carry this out. As a
result, church music with the accompaniment of wind instruments may
grow in importance.

Then there is the problem of space and the position of the organ and
choir, made more acute because of the vast amount of church building
caused by an ever-expanding population. Are we to continue to use the
choir loft for singers and organ, a feature that arose only in the Baroque
period, or will we return the organ or at least the schola to the sanctuary
where they belong? This is a question not only of liturgical propriety but
of acoustical practicality, especially if the congregation is to share in
the singing.

There is also the problem of church bells, which has won more consideration in recent years as an aid to religious observance. The combination
of tones in the several bells is as important as their proportional tone
and the materials from which they are cast. Much research must be done
in this field together with efforts to revive older methods of pealing or
change-ringing, so that once more the tower music may give becoming
expression to the invitation to worship and the character of the feast, as
in centuries past.

But the main task of church music is, and will always be, the proper
musical setting for worship, by artistic choral and congregational song,
in chant, classical polyphony and the music of the present. To deepen
liturgical experience is to make church music more genuine. This is the
path every creative effort must choose to follow.

Select Bibliography

This list has been restricted to books in English. For the serious student the books listed offer, for the most part, a more extended bibliography.

1. GENERAL MUSIC HISTORY

APEL, WILLI (ed.). *The Harvard Dictionary of Music*. Cambridge, Mass.: Harvard University Press, 1947, 1956.

BLOM, ERIC (ed.). *Grove's Dictionary of Music and Musicians*. 5th ed. New York: Macmillan, 1954.

DAVISON, ARCHIBALD T. and APEL, WILLI (eds.). *Historical Anthology of Music*. 2 vols. Cambridge, Mass.: Harvard University Press, 1949 & 1950. Rev. ed. 1959.

GARVIE, PETER (ed.). *Music and Western Man*. New York: Philosophical Library, 1958.

GROUT, DONALD. *A History of Western Music*. New York: W. W. Norton, 1960.

HADOW, W. H. (ed.). *Oxford History of Music*. 6 vols. London: Clarendon Press, 1901–1905. Pref. to 2nd ed. by P. C. Buck, 1929.

LANG, PAUL HENRY. *Music in Western Civilization*. New York: W. W. Norton, 1941.

PARRISH, CARL (ed.). *A Treasury of Early Music*. New York: W. W. Norton, 1958.

PARRISH, CARL and OHL, JOHN F. *Masterpieces of Music before 1750*. New York: W. W. Norton, 1951.

SACHS, CURT. *The Commonwealth of Art*. New York: W. W. Norton, 1946.

——— Rhythm and Tempo. New York: W. W. Norton, 1953.

SLONIMSKY, NICHOLAS (ed.). *Baker's Biographical Dictionary of Musicians*. 5th ed. rev. New York: G. Schirmer, 1958.

STRUNK, WILLIAM OLIVER. *Source Readings in Music History*. New York: W. W. Norton, 1950.

THOMPSON, OSCAR. *The International Cyclopedia of Music and Musicians*. 7th ed., rev. by N. SLONIMSKY. New York: Dodd, Mead & Co. 1956.

2. CHURCH MUSIC

AIGRAIN, RENÉ. *Religious Music*. Trans. C. MULCAHY. London : Sands & Co., 1931.

DICKINSON, EDWARD. *Music in the History of the Western Church*. New York: C. Scribner's Sons, 1927.

DOUGLAS, CHARLES WINFRED. *Church Music in History and Practice*. New York: C. Scribner's Sons, 1937.

NEMMERS, EDWIN E. *Twenty Centuries of Catholic Church Music*. Milwaukee: Bruce, 1949.

WEINMANN, KARL. *History of Church Music*. New York: F. Pustet, 1910.

3. PRE-GREGORIAN PERIOD

OESTERLY, W.O.E. *The Jewish Background of the Christian Liturgy*. Oxford, 1925.

WELLESZ, EGON. *A History of Byzantine Music and Hymnography*. Oxford, 1949.

WERNER, ERIC. *The Sacred Bridge*. New York: Columbia University Press, 1959.

4. GREGORIAN CHANT

APEL, WILLI. *Gregorian Chant*. Bloomington, Ind.: Indiana University Press, 1958.

PIERIK, MARIE. *The Song of the Church*. New York: Longmans, 1947.

WAGNER, PETER. *Introduction to the Gregorian Melodies*. Pt. I. Reprinted in *Caecilia*, vols. 84–85 (1957–1958).

WELLESZ, EGON. *Eastern Elements in Western Chants.* Byzantine Institute of America, Oxford, 1947.

5. MEDIEVAL PERIOD

APEL, WILLI. *The Notation of Polyphonic Music, 900–1600.* 4th ed. rev. and with commentary. Medieval Academy of American Publications No. 38. Cambridge, Mass.: Harvard University Press, 1949.
BUKOFZER, MANFRED F. *Studies in Medieval and Renaissance Music.* New York: W. W. Norton, 1950.
HUGHES, ANSELM (ed.). *Early Medieval Music up to 1300. The New Oxford History of Music.* Vol. II. London: Oxford University Press, 1954.
PARRISH, CARL. *The Notation of Medieval Music.* New York: W. W. Norton, 1957.
REESE, GUSTAVE. *Music in the Middle Ages.* New York: W. W. Norton, 1940.
WOOLDRIDGE, H. E. *Early English Harmony.* Vol. I. London: B. Quaritch, 1913.

6. RENAISSANCE PERIOD

MERRITT, A. TILLMAN. *Sixteenth Century Polyphony.* Cambridge, Mass.: Harvard University Press, 1939.
REESE, GUSTAVE. *Music in the Renaissance.* Rev. ed. New York: W. W. Norton, 1959.
See also section 5, above.

7. BAROQUE PERIOD

BUKOFZER, MANFRED F. *Music in the Baroque Era.* New York: W. W. Norton, 1947.

8. CLASSICAL PERIOD

HADOW, W. H. *The Viennese Period. The Oxford History of Music.* Vol. V. London: Oxford University Press, 1931.

9. ROMANTIC PERIOD

ABRAHAM, GERALD. *A Hundred Years of Music.* London: Duckworth, 1938.

EINSTEIN, ALFRED. *Music in the Romantic Era.* New York: W. W. Norton, 1950.

10. TWENTIETH CENTURY

DEMUTH, NORMAN. *Musical Trends in the Twentieth Century.* London: Rockliff, 1952.

SALAZAR, ADOLFO. *Music in Our Time.* Trans. by Isabel Pope. New York: W. W. Norton, 1946.

Composer Index

225

General Index